JOHN WHAITE BAKES

AT
Home

JOHN WHAITE BAKES

AT Home

headline

To Paul you are my world. To my family you are my home.

First published in 2014
by HEADLINE PUBLISHING GROUP

1

Cataloguing in Publication Data is available from the British Library

Hardback ISBN 9780755365128

Project Editor: Mari Roberts
Design and Art Direction: Smith & Gilmour Ltd
Photography: Matt Russell
Food Stylists: Richard Harris and Annie Rigg
Prop Stylist: Tamzin Ferdinando
Typeset in Scala and Alternate Gothic
Printed and bound in Italy by Rotolito Lombarda S.p.A

HEADLINE PUBLISHING GROUP
An Hachette UK Company
338 Euston Road, London NW1 3BH
www.headline.co.uk
www.hachette.co.uk

CONTENTS

INTRODUCTION

At home is where our baking stories most often begin. In our own kitchen, surrounded by evocative smells and familiar faces, we experiment with flavours and techniques. We play our favourite music as we whip cream or melt chocolate, and the soothing rhythm of creation takes hold. We are safe. We *feel* safe.

After creation, comes pleasure. I adore gobbling down a dessert, but the biggest pleasure I derive is seeing my family's and friends' faces as they serenely and silently relish the bake of the week. And the fact that this was created in my own home – well, there can't be a greater sense of comfort and safety.

Perhaps that's why so many of us bake throughout our entire lives: it enables us to spend quality time with those we love, be they friends or family, in our own homes – or wherever we feel most at home. I honestly don't believe that 'home' is restricted to that one place you return to in the evening, with your own colour schemes and ornaments adorning the walls. Anywhere I can unwrap my knife kit, beat some butter and sugar, and just bake, is a form of home for me.

On a Friday night, for instance, when we are set free from the constraints of our working lives and let loose, my group of friends and I get together to eat, drink and generally be merry. Although the location of our weekly meets and eats alters from one Friday to the next, there is always an almost tangible feeling of homeliness. My good friends recently moved into their first house. It was a building site for many weeks, but that didn't stop us from cosily convening on cardboard boxes, bowls of pudding in our laps and pies in our hands. These friendship feasts aren't confined to a single location, but can – and do – happen anywhere there is food available,

and good quality, homemade food at that.

Home doesn't have to be an abundance of fairy lights and friends. It can also be a moment of time alone, or that all-too-common feeling of a rumbling tum that awakens us in the night. The feeling that forces us to sneak downstairs in peckish pursuit of a midnight feast or an indulgent treat. That too, although a time of solitude, has a haunting homeliness.

The times I spend baking in my home are the very best. The looks on my nephews' and nieces' faces when we bake together, as they try to roll pastry that sticks stubbornly to their rolling pins, add an extra special something to my life. Even those rushed grab-'n'-go breakfasts, and the rare leisurely brunches and lunches with a partner, are times to be relished, and memories in the making. And then there are the special occasions: Christmas, Halloween, weddings. All are moments of indulgence and celebration with those people who make us feel most at home.

Many people have asked me why I am writing a book about home baking when I'm fresh from a patisserie diploma. Well, I could write a book on patisserie, or a book on bakes from around the world, but I'm not ready yet. I wanted to create a book that celebrated the simplicity of baking and the true meaning of home. That's not to say these recipes are slapdash simple – they aren't. Some of them employ techniques I learned in my recent baking education; some of them show off new favourite flavour combinations; all of them are treats that I would serve my family and friends at home. So, choose a recipe, relish the time you spend creating something delicious, and, more importantly, savour the time you spend with your loved ones. The food might only last a few greedy minutes, but the memories will last a lifetime.

RECIPE FINDER

BEFORE YOU START

First things first, just to ensure that we – you and I both – start off on the same foot.

EGG AND SPOON

All eggs are large; I prefer to use free-range
1 tsp = 5ml
1 tbsp = 15ml

SUGAR

I use unrefined, such as golden caster, in my baking. If you want white meringues, though, use a refined white caster sugar for those.

OVENS

I've given temperatures for conventional ovens, fan ovens and gas ovens. I have a fan oven, and so the temperature I use is the middle one. If your oven is on the hot or cool side, then adjust the temperature accordingly. An internal oven thermometer is a godsend, and inexpensive; oven thermostats are often misleading or inaccurate.

A good way of testing the temperature of an oven if you don't have an oven thermometer is to bake a 20cm/8-inch Victoria sponge. At 180°C/160°C fan/Gas 4, this should take 20–22 minutes. If, after this time, the cake domes in the centre and the edges are a little crispy, then your oven is on the hot side and you should reduce the temperature you use by just a few degrees. If the cake is still raw in the middle, and a skewer inserted into the centre comes out with batter sticking to it, then you need to adjust your oven temperature upwards for baking.

Gas ovens are a different kettle of fish altogether. I find they tend to burn cakes on the outside and leave them raw in the middle. If you use a gas oven, you need to know its quirks.

KITCHEN TIPS

READING A RECIPE AND PREPARING

Whether you're a baking newbie or an expert baking granny, it always pays to read the recipe through. Not only does this pattern the recipe out in your mind, but it also allows you to ensure you have everything you need before you're halfway through.

When it comes to making the dish, I always start by weighing all the ingredients out in true TV chef style. That's not out of habit, but out of fear – knowing my clumsiness, if I didn't weigh the ingredients before I started, I might get to the final stage of a recipe only to discover I've missed something fundamental out. Also, when you've got the ingredients in front of you, you can group them into stages, and that can save you time.

PREPARING BAKING TINS

Most new bakeware is excellently and reliably non-stick. If, however, you've fallen foul of bakeware with stubborn sticking qualities, then this is a foolproof way to get round it. Paint the tin liberally with melted butter. Put it into the freezer for 10 minutes or so for the butter to set, then paint it again with more butter. Return the tin to the freezer until needed, then, just before you add the mixture to be baked, dust the tin with a light sifting of flour.

SOFTENING BUTTER

Sometimes recipes call for 'softened butter', which essentially means not using it straight from the fridge, when it will be too hard to beat and cream. But if you live in quite a cold, creaky house, just leaving it out at room temperature for a while won't cut it – especially in winter, or sometimes even in that constant disappointment we call summer. What I do is to put the block of butter between two sheets of baking paper and hammer it flat with a rolling pin – being careful not to tear the paper. I then massage it with my fingers and fists until it has softened.

TO SIFT OR NOT TO SIFT?

Some cake recipes say to sift the flour and others just say to throw the flour into the mixture, and it can be confusing. Nowadays, flour tends to be so well ground that there isn't much need to sift it to disperse large clumps. If, however, you've had your flour open in the cupboard for a long time, say, more than a month, I would give it a little sift just to check there aren't any nasties in there. The only time I instruct sifting of the flour is when it is being added to a very delicate batter, such as the Japanese Cotton Cheesecake on page 209.

PORTIONING THICK, STICKY PRODUCTS

A tablespoon of honey or a teaspoon of golden syrup can be a nightmare to get accurately on to a spoon, then off again and into the mixing bowl. The best way is to have a mug of just-boiled water by your side, dip the measuring spoon into the water, then, holding the spoon over your mixing bowl, pour in the syrup or honey, which will fall straight off. Dip the spoon in the water before every addition of syrup. If pouring treacle or golden syrup straight from a can, stand the can in some recently boiled water for a few minutes – this will help to make the syrup runnier, therefore easier to pour.

FOLDING, BEATING, WHISKING AND STIRRING

When I first started baking and following recipes, I would get confused and stressed by all the different terms. I thought the terms all had much the same meaning, but there are differences – even if they are almost immeasurably subtle.

Folding is the method of incorporation that helps to avoid deflating a batter or mixture. The best tool to use is a thin silicone spatula, or large, fairly flat metal spoon. Scrape the mixture round the edge of the bowl, then cut through the centre and fold some of the mixture up and on top of the rest. Folding doesn't have to be a slow and delicate operation; so long as the motion is correct, the speed can be as fast as you like.
Beating is a more vigorous, carefree motion. Ordinarily you'd beat eggs to break them up, but some batters need beating, especially those 'one-mix' batters where the incorporation and retention of air isn't necessarily a requirement.
Whisking is obviously done with a whisk, with either electric power or elbow power. This is the incorporation of air into an ingredient or mixtures such as cream and eggs, which will retain the air and often double or triple in volume. Whisking can be done in a freestanding electric mixer with whisk attachment, but keep your attention on it to avoid over-whisking the product, especially cream. Do note that a whisk can be used to stir too, as detailed below.
Stirring is a movement in between the vigorous beating and the gentle folding. It is the movement of a product, mixture or batter so as to mix and amalgamate, or to help distribute heat evenly. Crème pâtissière and curd are stirred to distribute heat in this way. A whisk, whilst its main use is to whisk as detailed above, can also be used to stir, as is the case with crème pâtissière. It enables a swifter stirring than a wooden spoon because it doesn't cause the mixture to lap against the sides of the bowl/pan and spill out.

STAGES OF WHISKING

When whipping cream or egg white, there are certain stages that are described by particular terms. Some people take these to be artistic descriptions, but in fact they are technical ones – though don't get too bogged down by technicalities.
Soft peak This is when the egg white or cream just holds a shape, so when you dip the whisk into it and pull it out again, the ingredient forms a little hump – not even a peak, really.

Medium peak As above, but this is a peak, albeit a limp one that almost flops back on itself.
Stiff peak As above, but, as the name suggests, the egg white or cream stands proud, completely upright in a firm peak.

HOW TO FILL A PIPING BAG

Put the piping bag into a large jug or vase and open the larger end up. Scoop the mixture into the piping bag, then twist the large end so that the mixture is forced towards the nozzle part.

FILLING CUPCAKE CASES AND PUDDING MOULDS

The best method I have found is to put the cupcake batter into a piping bag. That makes it much easier to portion into the moulds. Then, when it comes to finishing off the leftover batter, you can squeeze it into your waiting mouth ...

PERFECT PORTIONING OF COOKIE DOUGH

I love making cookies, not least because I get to use my 30ml (2 tbsp)-capacity ice-cream scoop with its spring-action handle. It makes for perfect portions, and a quick and easy dough release. If you don't have one, then it works just as well to weigh the entire dough. Divide this weight by the number of cookies the recipe makes. Weigh out each cookie, roll into a ball, and on to the sheet for baking.

AVOIDING SPLIT CAKE BATTER – DOES IT MATTER?

It doesn't really matter. The reason cake batter splits is because the butter and eggs aren't the same temperature and the two fats cannot emulsify. People think that if the cake batter splits, the cake won't be light and fluffy, but this isn't the case; in the oven, everything reaches the same temperature and blends together. Another myth surrounding split cake batter is that adding a tablespoon or so of flour will solve it. What the flour does is thicken the mixture and so 'masks' the split, but it doesn't merge the fats together. The best way to deal

with a split batter, if it concerns you, is to mix the cake batter in a heatproof bowl, and, if splitting occurs, set the bowl over a pan of barely simmering water and keep whisking. That helps to bring everything together.

SINKING CAKE SYNDROME

A cake sinking in the middle can be the result of too much of something, making it rise too high in the oven, then sink as it cools. The most common 'too muchness' is of baking powder or bicarbonate of soda. If you add too much of these chemical raising agents, the reaction between acid and alkaline creates an abundance of bubbles. In the heat of the oven, the bubbles expand so much that the cake cannot hold itself up any more and, weakened, it collapses when removed from the heat. The second factor in this rising rampage is too much mechanical aeration, that is to say you've over-whisked the butter and sugar, or got too much air into the eggs, which expands beyond return in the heat of the oven.

GANACHES

A ganache is an emulsion of warm cream and chocolate, which results in a smooth, shiny and, most importantly, decadent icing or frosting.
Setting a ganache I recommend pouring a freshly made ganache on to a baking tray or a heatproof plate. This increases the surface area and enables a quicker, more even set.
Ganache too firm If you have left a ganache for too long and it is too stiff to use, simply place the baking tray or heatproof plate into a very low oven for 30-second bursts to soften it gently.
Fridge? Unless the recipe says so, putting ganache in the fridge is not recommended. Not only does it chill it too quickly, often rendering it useless, but it will cause it to dull and lose its glossy shine.

MASKING A CAKE

When you want a cake to look ultra neat, it's a good idea to 'mask' it: cover it in a layer of buttercream, ganache, icing or frosting. Masking a cake isn't easy, but with a little patience, it can be done. Three tools are very useful. First, an offset (or 'crank-handled') palette knife – this allows you to spread the covering on the cake with even pressure. Secondly, a 'builder's set square', which you can buy cheaply at most DIY stores, and which enables you to get a smooth top and sides. Finally, a cake turntable, which means the cake revolves easily, rather than you trying to twist yourself around it.

A chilled cake is easier to mask, as it becomes more stable and less susceptible to crumbling, though admittedly some cakes become too dry when chilled. Place the cake, or cake half, on to a cake board of the same (or just slightly larger) diameter. Dollop a generous amount of the ganache or buttercream on top, then gently spread it out towards the edges of the cake and manipulate it down the sides. Once you have the top as neat and flat as possible, use the builder's square: place its right angle against the cake board and gently scrape it around the cake and then across the top to make an ultra smooth mask. Chill the cake for a few minutes, then use any remaining ganache or buttercream to repeat the process and get the masking ultra neat.

TEMPERING CHOCOLATE

Tempered chocolate is useful for when you need chocolate to snap and shine. Sometimes, simply melting and re-setting chocolate isn't enough, because it doesn't set hard, and 'blooms' easily: goes a funny grey colour. Tempering controls how the crystals produced in the cocoa butter set, with the aim of achieving a high-shine, brittle result. There are a few different methods for tempering chocolate, but some of those are messy, and if like me you're not perfect at keeping things in the bowl, then it's best to avoid some of them for fear of looking as though you barely survived an explosion in a chocolate factory – one can only dream of such things.

Start by placing the chocolate in a heatproof bowl. Set this over a pan of barely simmering water and allow it to melt slowly. You don't need to stir it or disturb it in any way; just let it melt. The longer it takes to melt here the better.

When the chocolate has melted and runs freely from a spoon, remove the bowl from the heat and place it in a bigger bowl containing water and ice. With a spatula, stir the chocolate constantly over this ice bath, scraping the chocolate as it thickens from the sides – this takes elbow grease, believe me. After about 3 minutes, take the bowl from the ice bath and keep stirring. If the mixture doesn't thicken, place the bowl back in the ice bath, stirring all the time – you want the mixture to thicken to the consistency of a chocolate spread. If the mixture goes any thicker than this, it will still work, but more attention will be required at the next stage.

Place the thickened chocolate back over the heat, stirring vigorously and constantly, for just a few seconds, then remove and stir. If the chocolate doesn't come back to a melted consistency, return to the heat and stir again for another few seconds, then remove. Keep doing this until the chocolate is almost melted, then remove from the heat and stir vigorously, flattening any unmelted chunks as though you are trying to spread them. You don't want the chocolate to become too hot and runny, so only heat it for a tiny amount of time each go, and give it a stir for a good minute off the heat so that the residual heat is dispersed. If the chocolate starts to set in the bowl, hold it over the heat for a few seconds and stir until smooth.

Test the chocolate – so many people don't test the chocolate and so when they come to use it they make a right old mess. Drizzle a little bit on to the back of a palette knife or spoon, which should be at room temperature, and leave it to one side. If within a few minutes the chocolate starts to thicken and set, then it is tempered. If the chocolate is still tacky and melted, then I'm afraid you have to start again. Ordinarily temperatures are measured for each stage, but that is pointless for small amounts of chocolate because a thermometer will not keep up with the rate of changing temperatures and will give you a false reading. Just remember the texture the chocolate should be at each stage:

1 melted;
2 cooled to a spreadable consistency;
3 warmed back to melted, but not too hot or too runny.

CARAMEL METHODS

Making caramel is not difficult, it just takes some attention. There are two main ways of making caramel: dry and wet. Wet is the easiest as the sugar is dissolved in water first and then heated; dry is made without water and is a little trickier. With a wet caramel, you must never stir at any point, whereas with a dry caramel, stirring is a vital part of the process.

Wet Place the recipe's amount of sugar and water into a saucepan of an appropriate size. Place over a medium-high heat and allow to boil away until the mixture starts to brown. Swirl the pan gently, and allow the caramel to colour to a golden amber or dark amber, depending on the recipe. To stop it darkening, you can plunge the base of the pan into a bowl of cold water.

Dry Place a saucepan on a high heat and allow to warm up slightly. Sprinkle a quarter of the sugar into the pan and allow to melt to a clear liquid with just a few lumps; add another quarter and stir a little with a heatproof spatula until it has melted; then add another quarter and repeat, before adding the final quarter. When all of the sugar has dissolved, the mixture should be fairly pale amber, so allow to colour to either golden or dark, then plunge the pan into cold water. Use the caramel as required.

TYPES OF MERINGUE

There are three different types of meringue that I love to use.

Traditional This is the no-fuss method of whisking egg whites until they are at a medium-stiff peak, then slowly incorporating the sugar as the mixer whisks on a medium speed, until the meringue is glossy and holds its shape in a stiff peak. Once baked this can have a craze-inducing crisp outside, with a billowy and marshmallowy inside. Some bakers choose to put cream of tartar and vinegar into the unbaked meringue, but I don't faff about in such a way. Just two ingredients make for the perfect meringue.

Italian This is a little trickier, but is best for when you need to use a meringue on something like a lemon meringue pie. Because the eggs in the meringue 'batter' are cooked by the heat of the sugar syrup which is slowly added into the whisking eggs, this can be eaten unbaked.

Swiss Probably the trickiest to get quite right. Egg whites and sugar are whisked constantly and vigorously by hand over a water bath of simmering water, until the mixture feels quite hot on the finger. The mix is then transferred into a free-standing electric mixer with whisk attachment and whisked on high speed until back to room temperature. This can also be done using a handheld electric mixer, but it takes longer. This meringue 'batter' is so stiff that when turned upside down it should hold even the whisk attachment in place. The result, once baked, is powdery and crisp, like you'd expect to find in an old-fashioned bakery.

HOW TO KNEAD DOUGH

Often the most important part of bread making is in the kneading. If you don't develop the gluten, the finished bake will lack structure and strength, and will be dense and doughy. That's not to say, though, that you have to spend hours battling with stubborn dough. There are a few different kneading techniques that work particularly well. Remember that to develop the gluten from the proteins in the flour, you need to keep stretching the dough. So whether you follow one of the methods below, or a method of your own, if you're stretching the dough, you're doing the right thing.

The continental 'slap and fold' It sounds like a dodgy dance you might perform on an 18–30 holiday, but it is actually a fabulous, and easy, way of kneading bread. It works particularly well for wetter, stickier dough, especially enriched doughs packed with butter and eggs. With the dough in front of you, slowly sticking itself to the countertop, scoop your fingers under it, lift it up, then quite vigorously flip it over, slap it down, then fold it in half. Repeat this motion for about 10 minutes, or until the dough slowly stops sticking to the counter, and is smooth and elastic.

The famer's wife's kneading technique This isn't the 'technical' term, but rather a term

I use in humorous adoration of my mum. She's a farmer's wife, but she never really makes much bread, and when she does, she just prods and pushes the dough, pinny on and sleeves rolled up, getting redder and redder in the cheek as she kneads. This is a better technique for dryer doughs, which won't stretch and yield to the continental method. With the heel of your palm gently stretch the dough away from you, then with your fingers roll it back up into a ball. Repeat this motion, stretching the dough away and rolling it back, until it is smooth and elastic. Again, this should take about 10 minutes.

Dough hook Of course, if you have a freestanding electric mixer with a dough hook attachment, simply use that on a medium speed. It usually takes around 5–7 minutes to knead a dough with this method, but do still check using the methods below.

IS MY DOUGH SUFFICIENTLY KNEADED?

Telling when your dough is ready is vital. So often people give the dough a quick prod, then chuck it in a bowl to rise without checking whether or not it's at the right stage. The two best methods are:

The window-pane test Cover your fingers in plenty of flour. Rip a small, walnut-sized chunk of dough off, then gently try to stretch it out, using even pressure over the full chunk of dough. This isn't a rigorous quick stretch, but a gentle 'pulling' of the dough. If you can pull it out thin enough to see light through it, without the dough tearing, then you're there.

The poke test Roll the dough into a tight ball. With a well-floured finger, poke the dough gently. If the dough rises up again and the poke disappears, the dough is ready.

RAPID DOUGH PROVING

The patience required in proving bread results in a gorgeous, malty ferment flavour. That said, however, there are times when I just want my bread and I want it quick. This is particularly the case when the recipe has strongly flavoured ingredients in it, and so the bread doesn't necessarily need to have an emboldened tang in its own right. My method for rapid dough proving is to roll the ball of dough in oil and place it into an oiled bowl, turn the electric oven light on – but with no heat – and place a tray of just boiled water at the bottom of the oven. This creates a moist, warm environment, which is absolutely perfect for yeast to get working. The amount of time it takes your dough to double in size will depend on the temperature of the environment and strength of the yeast, but for my doughs, instead of an hour at room temperature, this method takes about 30 minutes.

I don't recommend you prove Danish dough in this way; the heat of the oven and the humidity can melt the buttery layers.

HOW PUFF PASTRY WORKS

Puff pastry, or laminated pastry, be it rough puff or full puff, is when the pastry dough has been folded up in a specific way with fat, normally butter, in between the layers. Those seams of fat, when introduced to the heat of the oven, melt, turn to steam, and force the layers of dough apart. The best way to achieve an optimum rise from pastry is to put it in the oven at a lower temperature, about 200°C/180°C fan/Gas 6, which allows the butter to melt without the dough layers stiffening, then to turn the heat up by 20 degrees to create a blast of steam, and to firm the dough layers.

FAST FABULOUS BREAKFASTS

Stumbling out of bed and jumping into the kitchen just to pour a few dried flakes of something into a bowl is not my idea of fun. I mean, breakfast is such an important meal, why get it out of a cardboard box? In the morning, I like to have food that is worth waking up for. I'm not being unrealistic here – I know people don't have hours to spend in the morning doing breakfast bakes – so most of these recipes are ones that can be made in advance and then put away to await your morning hunger.

BLOOD ORANGE AND ALMOND TARTLETS
MAKES 8

For the almond cream
Zest 2 medium blood oranges
50g unsalted butter, softened
50g golden caster sugar
Small pinch of salt
1 egg
½ tsp almond extract
50g ground almonds
1 tbsp plain flour

To assemble
1 quantity Rough Puff Pastry
    (see page 246) or 500g shop-
    bought all-butter puff pastry
1 egg, beaten with a pinch
    of salt, to glaze
2 blood oranges from above
1 tbsp icing sugar

For the glaze
1 tbsp apricot jam
2 tsp water

Essential equipment
9cm /3½-inch cookie cutter
7cm /2¾-inch cookie cutter
Piping bag fitted with 2cm
    plain nozzle
Baking sheet lined with
    a sheet of baking paper

I adore pastry – that's no secret – but even I can sometimes be a little too full, or it can be a little too early in the day, to cope with something heavy and overly sweet. These tartlets make a perfect breakfast snack, because the tang of the orange balances the sweet almond cream perfectly. Blood oranges have a short season – January to March. If out of season, use regular, medium oranges instead.

1 Preheat the oven to 200°C/180°C fan/Gas 6.

2 First, make the almond cream. In a mixing bowl, beat together the zest, butter, sugar and salt until paler in colour and fluffy in texture. Add the egg and almond extract and beat those in too, then fold in the ground almonds and flour. Set aside until needed.

3 Flour the worktop and a rolling pin, and roll out the pastry until it is about 3mm thin. Cut out 16 discs of pastry using the larger cookie cutter. Using the smaller cookie cutter, cut out the centre of 8 of the discs, so that you have 8 full discs and 8 pastry rings. Glaze the top of the full discs with a little of the beaten egg, then stick the pastry rings on top, like a large, flat vol-au-vent shell. (The remaining pastry can be layered up and frozen to be used for something else.)

4 Peel the oranges. The best way to do this neatly is to trim the bottom, then sit the orange upright. With a sharp knife, slice between the flesh and the pith,

BLOOD ORANGE AND ALMOND TARTLETS CONTINUED

from top to bottom, rotating the orange as you go until perfectly free of peel and pith. Then slice each one into 6 discs about 1cm deep. Keep the four inner discs, and discard – i.e. eat – the two smaller, top and bottom ones.

5 Place the almond cream in the piping bag and pipe a good blob into the centre of the prepared tart cases, though don't flatten it out – it will spread in the heat of the oven. Place the slices of orange on top of the almond cream; the slices should be slightly smaller than the hole in the top ring of pastry. Glaze the pastry ring, then sift a heavy fall of icing sugar over the entire surface – orange and all – of each tart.

6 Arrange well spaced on the lined baking sheet, and bake for 5 minutes, then turn the heat up to 220°C/200°C fan/Gas 7 and bake for a further 15 minutes.

7 Meanwhile, make the glaze: heat the jam and water in a saucepan until just boiling, then remove from the heat and mix well. As soon as the tarts come out of the oven, arrange on a wire rack, and paint each one liberally with the apricot glaze. Allow to cool completely before serving.

CHILLI, SAFFRON AND SPELT LOAF

MAKES 1 SMALL LOAF

100ml milk
Generous pinch of
 saffron strands
200g white bread flour
100g spelt flour
7g salt
7g sachet fast-action yeast
110ml water, straight from
 the tap
2 tbsp olive oil
100g green pickled chillies,
 drained and roughly chopped

Essential equipment
450g/1lb loaf tin, greased

When breakfast time arrives (never soon enough, I have to add), I often crave something immensely savoury with a bit of a kick. This loaf is really great for that. I like to toast a slice, and top it with melted cheese and a poached egg – a sort of ad hoc rarebit.

1 Place the milk and saffron in a small saucepan, set over a low heat and allow to infuse for a good 10 minutes.

2 Meanwhile, mix together the flours and the salt, then stir the yeast in. When the saffron has turned the milk a glorious golden yellow, add the water and olive oil, then pour this into the flours and bring together into a scraggy ball. Turn out on to the counter top and knead for about 10 minutes, or until smooth and elastic. If you have a freestanding electric mixer, use the dough attachment to knead, which will take about 5 minutes.

3 Place the dough into an oiled or floured bowl and allow to rise until doubled in size: between 1 and 2 hours at room temperature.

4 Preheat the oven to 220°C/200°C fan/Gas 7.

5 Place the dough on the counter and add the chillies. Slowly knead the dough to incorporate the chillies, then roll into a sausage the length of the dough tin. Place the dough into the tin and allow to rise until doubled in size again.

6 Bake the risen dough for 35–40 minutes, or until beautifully golden. Remove from the tin and allow to cool before slicing.

COFFEE AND WHITE CHOCOLATE CHIP MUFFINS
MAKES 12

170g salted butter, softened
100g icing sugar
70g light muscovado sugar
3 eggs
1 tsp vanilla bean paste
   or extract
1 tbsp freeze-dried coffee
   granules
1 tbsp milk
190g plain flour
2 tsp baking powder
125g white chocolate chips

For the topping
200g thick Greek yoghurt
125g icing sugar
1 tsp freeze-dried
   coffee granules
1 tsp milk

Essential equipment
Disposable piping bag
12-hole deep muffin tray,
   lined with muffin cases

Coffee is most people's best friend in the morning. I like to sit and stare into space with a big mug of coffee before I start the day. Some mornings, though, when I've had the audacity to 'snooze' my alarm clock for an hour, I have to slip out of bed, into my clothes and out of the door. So a batch of these, made the night before, is the perfect solution to emergency morning madness.

1 Preheat the oven to 200°C/180°C fan/Gas 6.

2 Place the butter into a bowl and beat until smooth, then add the icing sugar and brown sugar, and beat until the sugar has dissolved into the butter and is smooth and light. Beat in the eggs and vanilla until well incorporated.

3 Dissolve the coffee granules in the milk, then beat that in too.

4 Add the flour and baking powder, beat in until just incorporated, and then fold through the chocolate chips.

5 Scoop the mixture into the disposable piping bag, snip a large hole in the end, then divide equally amongst the holes in the muffin tray.

6 Bake for 20–25 minutes, or until a skewer inserted into the centre comes out clean. Allow to cool completely.

7 To make the topping, simply beat the yoghurt and icing sugar together. Dissolve the coffee in the milk and beat that in too. Chill to firm, then dollop on to the muffins when ready to serve.

STICKY GINGER MUFFINS

MAKES 12

170g salted butter, softened
70g icing sugar
100g light muscovado sugar
3 eggs
1 tsp vanilla bean paste
  or extract
2 tsp ground ginger
3 tbsp golden syrup
190g plain flour
2 tsp baking powder
3 balls stem ginger,
  very finely chopped

For the topping
100g icing sugar
1 tsp syrup from stem
  ginger jar

Essential equipment
Disposable piping bag
12-hole deep muffin tray,
  lined with muffin cases

My absolute favourite of all muffins. The stickiness and stodginess of these, as well as that gentle tongue-tickling heat, is perfect first thing. Make the night before, ready for the morning.

1 Preheat the oven to 200°C/180°C fan/Gas 6.

2 Place the butter into a bowl and beat until smooth, then add the icing sugar and brown sugar, and beat until the sugar has dissolved into the butter and is smooth and light.

3 Beat in the eggs, vanilla, ginger and golden syrup until well mixed. Add the flour and baking powder, beat in until just incorporated, and then fold through the stem ginger.

4 Scoop the mixture into the disposable piping bag, snip a large hole in the end, then divide equally amongst the holes in the muffin tray.

5 Bake for 20–25 minutes, or until a skewer inserted into the centre comes out clean. Allow to cool completely.

6 To make the topping, simply beat the icing sugar and stem ginger syrup together until the icing is pourable, but not too runny. You may need a little extra icing sugar, or syrup, to adjust the consistency. Spoon over the cold muffins and serve.

GRAPE-AND-GO DANISHES
MAKES 8

1 quantity Rough Puff Danish
  Pastry (see page 248)
1 egg, beaten with a pinch
  of salt, to glaze
½ quantity Cardamom Crème
  Pâtissière (see page 252)
24 red grapes
8 tsp apricot jam

Essential equipment
1–2 baking sheets, greased
  and lined with baking paper
Disposable piping bag, with
  end snipped off to create
  a 1cm hole

Made the night before, these make for a brilliant grab-and-go breakfast, so long as you have a coffee to go too! If you are not a fan of cardamom, use the recipe for plain crème pâtissière instead, but believe me when I declare that grape and cardamom make for an exquisite flavour combination.

1 Lightly flour a rolling pin and worktop and roll out the pastry to about 30 × 33cm. Trim the edges to neaten, and then slice into 8 equal rectangles. Glaze about 3mm of the edge of the pastry, then fold 5mm of the corners in and press to seal, and fold over about 5mm of the straight edges, pressing lightly to seal. You should end up with a slice shaped like a rough jewel. Continue with the other seven, and set them on the baking sheet/s, evenly spaced apart.

2 Load the crème pâtissière into the piping bag, and pipe a line down the centre of each pastry portion. Slice the grapes in half down the longest part, then lay them across the crème pâtissière, overlapping them slightly.

3 Allow the slices to prove until they are swollen and tremble when the baking sheet is gently nudged. Preheat the oven to 220°C/200°C fan/Gas 7, and gently glaze the edges of the pastry slices with the beaten egg. Bake in the oven for 20–25 minutes, or until gloriously golden.

4 Whilst the slices bake, heat the jam with 2 tbsp water in a small saucepan over a high heat. When it starts to boil, strain it into a clean bowl. When the slices come out of the oven, use a pastry brush to glaze the grapes and crème pâtissière generously with the jam.

LEMON AND POPPY SEED MUFFINS
MAKES 12

170g salted butter, softened
70g icing sugar
100g golden caster sugar
Zest of 3 lemons
3 eggs
1 tsp vanilla bean paste
  or extract
6 tbsp poppy seeds
170g plain flour
2 tsp baking powder

For the topping
50g golden caster sugar
50ml water
Juice of 1 lemon
Poppy seeds to sprinkle

Essential equipment
Disposable piping bag
12-hole deep muffin tray,
  lined with muffin cases

The recipe for Lemon and Poppy Seed Scones in my first book was so popular that I thought I'd continue that favourite flavour combination with these breakfast muffins. Not only is the lemon perfectly zesty and awakening in the morning, but the poppy seeds seem to pop in the mouth and deliver a perfect morning bite. These are perfectly fine made the night before, cooled, then stored in an airtight container.

1 Preheat the oven to 200°C/180°C fan/Gas 6.

2 Place the butter into a bowl and beat until smooth, then add the icing sugar, caster sugar and zest, and beat until the sugar has dissolved into the butter and is smooth and light.

3 Beat in the eggs, vanilla and poppy seeds until well mixed. Sift over the flour and baking powder, and fold in until just incorporated.

4 Scoop the mixture into the disposable piping bag, snip a large hole in the end, then divide equally amongst the holes in the muffin tray.

5 Bake for 20–25 minutes, or until a skewer inserted into the centre comes out clean. Allow to cool completely.

6 To make the topping, simply heat the sugar and water in a small saucepan. Allow to boil and the sugar to dissolve, then remove from the heat and stir in the lemon juice. Paint the warm syrup over the muffins using a pastry brush, and then top each one with a generous sprinkle of poppy seeds.

APPLE AND GRANOLA BREAKFAST CAKE

SERVES 12–16

225g butter, softened
225g light brown soft sugar
1 tsp vanilla bean paste
  or extract
4 eggs
225g plain flour
1 tsp baking powder
2 apples, peeled, cored and
  chopped to 1cm cubes
200g granola, reserve some
  for topping

Essential equipment
23cm/9-inch square cake
  tin, greased and lined with
  baking paper

Softened apples buried deep inside a pudding-like cake, with crispy crumbs of granola – definitely something worth waking up for. I often make this on a Friday night so I have something good to eat on a Saturday and Sunday morning. In the unlikely event you still have some left by Monday, toast it lightly under the grill.

1 Preheat the oven to 180°C/160°C fan/Gas 4.

2 Place the butter, sugar and vanilla into a mixing bowl and beat together until the butter and sugar are well mixed, and the mixture is fluffy.

3 Beat in the eggs, then the flour and baking powder. Finally, gently fold in the apple chunks and granola.

4 Scoop the mixture into the prepared baking tin and level off. Sprinkle over more granola, and bake for 40–50 minutes, or until a skewer inserted into the centre comes out clean.

CHERRY TEA ALL BRAN CAKE
SERVES 8–10

4 tea bags, such as
   English Breakfast
200ml hot water
200g All Bran
100ml milk
100g chopped prunes
150g kirsch-soaked
   cherries, drained
1 tsp vanilla bean paste
   or extract
175g light muscovado sugar
150g plain flour
1 tsp baking powder
4 tbsp Demerara sugar

Essential equipment
900g/2lb loaf tin, greased
   and lined

What a marvellous thing this is. One of the many cakes Mum used to make for me when I was a tot. The benefit of it then was its simplicity, so Mum could throw it together and into the oven, without me getting so bored that I'd scream the house down. The benefit of it these days is still very much that simplicity. Made the night before, this is even better the next morning, with a little softened butter. You'll note that this recipe contains no eggs and no butter. If it was for a totally dairy-free individual, then swap the milk for more hot water, and you have the ultimate treat.

1 Allow the teabags to infuse the water for 10 minutes, then squeeze out all of the moisture from the teabags. Put the All Bran into a mixing bowl with the tea and milk, chopped prunes, cherries, vanilla and sugar, and allow to soak for an hour.

2 Preheat the oven to 180°C/160°C fan/Gas 4.

3 Add the flour and baking powder to the mixture and stir well in. Scoop into the loaf tin, sprinkle over the Demerara sugar and bake for 35–40 minutes or until a skewer inserted into the centre comes out fairly clean.

CROISSANTS
MAKES 12

1 quantity Rough Puff Danish
  Pastry (see page 248)
1 egg, beaten with a pinch
  of salt, to glaze

Essential equipment
2 baking sheets, greased
2 large carrier bags
2 ramekins or cups

On the occasional Sunday I treat myself to three or four croissants, smothered in butter and sharp, blackcurrant jam. It takes a little work, so it is probably best to make them the day before. Baked croissants freeze well for up to three months. Defrost, then heat in an oven set to 180°C/160°C fan/Gas 4 for 12 minutes, or until crispy on the outside, and yielding when gently squeezed.

1 Flour the worktop and a rolling pin, roll out the pastry to a rectangle roughly 45 × 35cm, then trim to a neat 40 × 30cm. Divide in half lengthways, so you have two long rectangles of 40 × 15cm. Take one of these rectangles and cut out 6 triangles – I cut out one triangle, cut out an 'upside down' triangle, and so on. Repeat with the other rectangle of dough, so that you have 12 triangles in total.

2 Take one of the triangles of dough, stretch it out slightly, then roll it up, starting with the base of the triangle, rolling it up to the tip. Place this on a greased baking sheet with the tip underneath. Repeat with the remaining croissants; you should get 6 on each baking sheet. Place each baking sheet in a carrier bag, and put a ramekin of hot water into each bag – this creates a steamy environment, which not only prevents the croissants from crusting and drying out, but also helps the proving process.

3 Allow the croissants to prove until they are swollen and tremble like a thick jelly when the baking sheet is nudged. This can take anywhere between 1 and 3 hours, depending on the heat of the kitchen – don't try to speed this up with my 'rapid dough proving' hint on page 15, as this could melt the butter.

4 Preheat the oven to 200°C/180°C fan/Gas 6.

5 When the croissants have proved, glaze each one – gently, so as not to tear the dough – then bake for 25–30 minutes or until perfectly golden.

APPLE, MACADAMIA NUT AND OATMEAL COOKIES

MAKES 16–20

150g unsalted butter,
  softened
80g golden caster sugar
80g dark muscovado sugar
1 tsp vanilla bean
  paste or extract
1 egg
100g medium oatmeal
125g plain flour
1 tsp baking powder
100g dried apple, cut
  into small cubes
80g macadamia nuts,
  roughly chopped

Essential equipment
Baking sheet/s lined
  with baking paper

These inelegant cookies are nothing short of heaven-sent. The dried apples are chewy, the macadamia nuts crunchy, and the oatmeal adds great texture in between the two. I roll this dough into a thick sausage in cling film and chill it, slicing off 1cm(ish) slices to bake as and when the occasion demands. Let's face it, were I to bake these in a single batch they wouldn't last two minutes.

1 Put the butter and sugars into a mixing bowl and beat together until paler and fluffy – this can be done by hand with an electric mixer, or in a freestanding mixer with paddle attachment.

2 Add the vanilla and egg, beat until combined, then beat in the oatmeal, flour and baking powder – scraping the bowl with a spatula if necessary to bring the mixture off the sides. Fold in the apple and nuts, then scoop on to a length of cling film and roll into a sausage. Chill for 30 minutes.

3 Preheat the oven to 200°C/180°C fan/Gas 6. Cut off as many 1cm(ish) thick slices as you desire, arrange well spaced on the baking sheet/s and bake for 9–12 minutes, or until slightly darker around the edges. Remove from the oven and allow to cool.

FLUFFY GINGERBREAD PANCAKES
MAKES 8

150g self-raising flour
1 tsp baking powder
2–3 tsp ground ginger
1 tsp ground cinnamon
120ml milk
2 tsp black treacle
1 tsp golden syrup
2 eggs, separated

Essential equipment
Large frying pan or
  griddle pan

A day that begins with a pancake is sure to be a good day. These fluffy gingerbread pancakes not only taste like gingerbread and so are a sure-fire way of maintaining a good mood, but also, because they have both baking powder and whisked egg whites, they puff up to create the lightest, fluffiest pancake imaginable. These are delicious served with maple syrup, or even a generous glug of golden syrup. Prepare the batter the night before, leave it in the fridge in a jug, and come the morning you're ready to fry and gobble.

1 Into a mixing bowl, sift the flour, baking powder, ginger and cinnamon. In a separate bowl, beat the milk, treacle, golden syrup and egg yolks, until the treacle and syrup have dissolved into the milk. Add the dry ingredients to the wet, and beat together to make a smooth, though fairly thick, batter.

2 In a clean bowl, whisk the egg whites to stiff peaks, then fold these into the batter.

3 Heat a little oil in the frying pan or griddle over a medium heat, and allow the pan to get fairly warm. Spoon small ladlefuls of the batter on to the pan – I do about two or three at once. Allow the pancakes to gently fry for about 1 minute, and when the bubbles on the surface start to pop, leaving little holes, flip them over and fry for a minute more.

4 Stack the pancakes up and serve.

LEISURELY BRUNCHES

People rarely take the time to stop, sit and enjoy something indulgent or simply delicious. Demands of family and the buzz of business often mean grabbing something quick and easy. So on a day when I can leisurely put ingredients into a bowl and create something worthwhile at my own pace, well, that is a perfect day for me. That's not to say that these recipes are ones you can only make on those rare restful days; these can be prepared in advance and eaten in a rush too – though I do strongly recommend you devour them in peace.

BRUNCH CHOUX RINGS
MAKES 4

½ quantity Choux Pastry
(see page 246)
Icing sugar, to dust

For the filling
½ quantity Crème Pâtissière
(see page 252)
200ml double cream, whipped
to soft, floppy peaks
2 tbsp runny honey
Fruit of choice

Essential equipment
Baking sheet lined with
baking paper
9cm/3½-inch round
cookie cutter
2 piping bags, fitted
with 10mm nozzles

*Choux rings make a great brunch: the choux isn't
so heavy that it makes you feel sluggish, but it does
deliver a satisfactory feeling of full. The choice of fruit
to fill these with is yours, but I recommend you go
for a mixture of sweet and sharp.*

1 Preheat the oven to 200°C/180°C fan/Gas 6.

2 Draw around the cookie cutter on to the baking
paper to make 4 circles. Put the choux pastry into
one of the piping bags and pipe choux circles on to
the templates. Pipe a second ring of choux on the
inside of each ring, then pipe a third and final ring
on top of the first two, on the seam line where they
meet. Bake for 30 minutes. Remove from the oven
and allow to cool.

3 Scoop the crème pâtissière into a bowl and whisk it
vigorously to loosen it. Add the cream and honey and
fold in. Put the filling into the second piping bag.

4 Slice each choux ring in half horizontally and pipe
full of the crème pâtissière mixture. Top with the
fruit of your choice and then replace the choux ring
lid. Dust with icing sugar and serve.

APPLE AND BLACKBERRY BRIOCHE GALETTE
SERVES 8-10

For the brioche
250g white bread flour
5g salt
7g sachet fast-action yeast
30g golden caster sugar
150g egg (about 3)
20ml milk
125g unsalted butter, cubed

For the topping
½ quantity Crème Pâtissière
   (see page 252)
1 large apple (Braeburn or
   Cox is best)
10–15 large blackberries
1 egg, beaten with a tiny
   pinch of salt, to glaze
6 tbsp apricot jam
3 tbsp water
Icing sugar to dust

Essential equipment
Baking sheet of at least
   25 × 25cm/10 × 10 inches
Piping bag (optional)

I do love brioche at brunch. The feeling of guilt and pleasure in one go is almost too hard to bear, but I can just about cope as I sink my teeth into the cloud-like bread, topped with softened apples, tangy blackberries and glorious custard. The brioche, as always, needs to be prepared the night before.

1 Make the brioche dough. Place the flour and salt in a the bowl of a freestanding electric mixer fitted with a dough hook and blend together. Then add the yeast and sugar and blend that through too. Beat the eggs with the milk, and add to the bowl. Gently mix by hand before turning the mixer on so that the flour doesn't explode everywhere when the mixer starts. Knead on a medium speed for 15 minutes, until the dough is extremely stretchy. You can do this by hand, but the dough is intensely sticky, at least to begin with.

2 Slowly add the butter piece by piece, mixing still on medium. It should take around 5 minutes to incorporate the butter and, when done, allow the mixer to continue for about 5 minutes, until the dough is smooth, silky and very stretchy indeed.

3 Place the dough on a greased baking tray and wrap tightly with cling film. Leave in the fridge overnight.

4 Make the crème pâtissière following the instructions on page 252, allow to cool completely, and refrigerate until needed.

5 When the brioche dough has rested overnight, flour the worktop lightly, and then roll out the brioche into

a large disc about 25cm in diameter. Place this on a baking sheet. Remove the crème pâtissière from the fridge and place in a mixing bowl. With a wooden spoon, vigorously beat the crème pâtissière into a smooth custard.

6 Spread or pipe the crème pâtissière on to the brioche disc, leaving a good inch around the edge. Peel, core and quarter the apple, then slice it very finely – I use a mandolin slicer. Arrange on the crème pâtissière in a spiral pattern from the outside in. Dot the blackberries here and there. Gently crimp the edge by pulling a little pastry outwards, then sticking it back on just to the left. Repeat until the brioche is perfectly crimped all round.

7 Preheat the oven to 200°C/180°C fan/Gas 6.

8 Allow the brioche galette to rest until the edge has puffed up and almost doubled in size (between 45 minutes and 2 hours), then glaze the edge and bake for 25–30 minutes, or until the exposed brioche is a beautiful, deep golden colour.

9 Heat the jam and water, pass through a sieve and glaze the hot, freshly baked brioche. Cool, then finish with a generous dusting of icing sugar.

ORANGE AND CRANBERRY GIRDLE SCONES
MAKES 8

Flavourless oil, for frying
250g plain flour
250g wholemeal flour
10g baking powder
120g unsalted butter, cubed
100g golden caster sugar
150g dried cranberries
Zest of 2 large oranges
2 eggs
200–225ml buttermilk
(or use ½ natural yoghurt
and ½ milk with 1 tsp
lemon juice)

Essential equipment
Large cast-iron frying pan

If you shoot an arrow between scones and pancakes, you hit girdle scones. Orange and cranberry is one of my favourite flavour combinations, and perfect for these. Serve them, as I do, warm with clotted cream and cherry jam.

1 Dab a little kitchen paper into the oil and rub it on to the cast-iron frying pan. Place on a high heat. Once hot, reduce the heat to medium so it doesn't smoke the kitchen out.

2 Sift the flours and baking powder into a bowl to blend them, and also to remove the bran from the wholemeal flour. Rub the cubes of butter into the flour mixture until it resembles inelegant breadcrumbs. Stir in the sugar, cranberries and zest.

3 Beat the eggs into the buttermilk, then slowly pour into the dry mixture. I usually add three-quarters of the wet mixture, then gently bring it together, adding the remaining wet mixture if necessary. The dough should feel like a fairly stiff bread dough, and of course will be a little bit sticky. The best way to bring the dough together is to tip it out on to the work top, then ball it up: don't knead it, just gently push the ball once or twice to incorporate any stray bits of dough.

4 Pat the dough down into a thin disc, no more than 1cm thick, then with a sharp knife cut into 8 equal triangular slices. Place these – I do 2 at a time to avoid overcrowding – on to the heated frying pan and fry for about 4 minutes on each side, or until a deep brown all over.

FULL ITALIAN BRUNCH STRATA
SERVES 6–8

1 tsp olive oil
125g bacon lardons
300g Tuscan salsiccia, cut
  into 5mm-thick half-moons
1 red pepper, cut into
  1cm cubes
100g chestnut mushrooms
1 small red onion, cut into
  very fine half-moon slices
100g cherry tomatoes, halved
Small handful fresh basil,
  very finely chopped
1 fat red chilli, deseeded
  and finely chopped
400g ciabatta, cut into
  2.5cm cubes
125g mozzarella pearls
75g Parmesan cheese,
  finely grated
150ml milk
9 eggs
Salt and pepper

Essential equipment
Medium enamel roasting dish

A true brunch of lazy indulgence has to be something you prepare the night before and throw into an oven the next day, and this strata is just that. I found the sausage (salsiccia) in my local Italian deli. Its flavour is bold, peppery and smoky, and it adds an authentic Italian kick to this dish. You are free to use any sausage, but the bolder the flavour, the better the strata.

1 Heat the olive oil in a medium saucepan and set over a high heat. Add the lardons and the sausage and cook, stirring, for a few minutes until the fat has seeped out of the meat and into the pan. Reduce the heat and add the pepper, mushrooms and red onion and allow to soften for just a few minutes. Remove from the heat and add the tomatoes, basil and chilli, give the pan a good stir, and then allow to cool.

2 To layer the strata, place some of the bread cubes on the bottom of the roasting dish and add half of the meat mixture and half of the mozzarella pearls – dotting them here and there. Sprinkle over a third of the Parmesan, then repeat the process. You should have layers of: bread, meat and mozzarella; Parmesan; bread, meat and mozzarella; Parmesan, and a final layer of bread and a generous sprinkling of Parmesan.

3 Beat the milk with the eggs and a small pinch of salt – the Parmesan will be salty anyway – and a more generous pinch of pepper. Pour over the strata and allow the bread to soak up the liquid – don't be afraid to squish any stubborn chunks down into the mix. Cover and refrigerate overnight, or until needed.

4 Remove the strata from the fridge and preheat the oven to 200°C/180°C fan/Gas 6. Bake the strata for 30–40 minutes, or until crispy and bronzed on top.

LEBANESE LONE WOLF EGGS
SERVES 1

1 tbsp sunflower or olive oil
½ small red onion,
  finely chopped
1–2 garlic cloves, minced
½ fat red chilli, deseeded
  and finely chopped
1 tsp sumac
1 tsp smoked paprika
1 tsp ground cumin
1 tsp ground coriander
1 tbsp pomegranate molasses
Half a 400g can chopped
  tomatoes
Leaves from 2 sprigs fresh
  thyme
1 tbsp fresh coriander,
  roughly chopped
Salt and pepper
1–2 eggs
Flatbreads, to serve

Essential equipment
Small frying pan

My Lone Wolf's Baked Eggs from the first book was so popular with friends, family and followers that I wanted to have a version of the recipe in this book too, but one with a twist. This is a spiced tomato sauce, into which you crack an egg or two. It was inspired by a dish I had at one of my favourite places to eat: Honey & Co. in London. I just can't stop making it. Especially when I'm at my parents' house and can sit idly in the sunny garden, and dip soft flatbreads into this.

1 Heat the oil in the saucepan set over a medium heat. Add the onions with a pinch of salt to help draw the water out so that they soften nicely. Allow to soften for about 5 minutes, stirring once in a while, then add the garlic, chilli, sumac, paprika, cumin and coriander, and stir well so the onions are coated in the colourful spices. Stir in the pomegranate molasses and add the tomatoes. Bring to the boil, then reduce to a simmer and allow to gently bubble for about 5 minutes, or until the sauce is a little thicker.

2 Stir in the thyme, coriander and a little salt and pepper, then crack in the egg(s) and allow the whites to cook completely, and the yolks to remain runny and unctuous. Serve at once with the flatbreads.

SMOKED MACKEREL QUICHE
SERVES 8

1 quantity Shortcrust Pastry
    (see page 247), or 320g packet
    of ready-rolled shortcrust
200g Charlotte potatoes,
    sliced into 5mm-thick discs
200ml milk
2 eggs
30ml white wine
300ml whipping cream
Zest of ½ lemon
1 tbsp wholegrain mustard
Small handful fresh dill,
    finely chopped
1 tsp salt
1 tsp cracked black pepper
125g gherkins, finely chopped
280g smoked mackerel,
    skins and bones removed

Essential equipment
23–25cm/9–10-inch loose-
    bottomed flan tin

Whenever I am afforded a non-working brunch and able to slowly meander about the house, I crave exactly this. The gentle smokiness of the mackerel is harmonised by the dill and potatoes. I much prefer this served cool, as by then the flavours have fused together, though it is still utterly delicious served hot.

1 Preheat the oven to 200°C/180°C fan/Gas 6.

2 Roll out the pastry and line the flan tin, pressing the pastry well into the grooves of the tin. Line with baking paper and fill with baking beans or rice. Bake for 15 minutes, then remove the beans and paper and bake for 12 minutes.

3 After blind-baking the pastry, reduce the oven temperature to 180°C/160°C fan/Gas 4.

4 Place the sliced potatoes in a large pan of water and bring to the boil. Boil for 7 minutes, then drain and place to one side to cool slightly.

5 Make the filling by beating together the milk, eggs, wine, cream, zest, mustard, dill, salt and pepper, then stir in the gherkins. Flake the mackerel and fold that in too, together along with the potatoes.

6 Pour into the blind-baked pastry case and bake for 35–45 minutes, or until the filling has puffed up slightly, has turned a very gentle golden brown, and when you nudge the tin slightly, the middle is cooked through but provocatively trembles a little. Allow to cool slightly before removing from the tin, and serve.

BRUNCH BURRITO
SERVES 1

½ small red onion,
  finely chopped
50g chorizo sausage,
  cut into small cubes
¼ yellow pepper, sliced
  into thin strips
½ fat red chilli, deseeded and
  finely chopped (optional)
1 tsp sunflower or olive oil
2 eggs
Half a 400g can baked beans,
  sauce included
1 large flatbread or large
  flour tortilla

*This makes for a very quick but flavoursome brunch.
I often love something meaty and spicy in the morning,
and this hits the spot perfectly.*

1 Place a small frying pan over a high heat and allow
to warm up, before adding the onion, chorizo, pepper,
and chilli if using. Allow to heat through, tossing the
pan occasionally.

2 Meanwhile, make an omelette by heating a larger
frying pan. Add the oil. Beat the eggs in a cup, then
add to the hot, oiled frying pan, and fry, jiggling the
pan back and forth, for a few minutes until your
omelette is cooked through. Slide it from the pan
and on to a plate.

3 When the chorizo mixture has cooked, add the
beans and allow to warm through.

4 To assemble, roll the omelette up and place it
in the centre of the flatbread. Pile the chorizo-bean
mix over the omelette, then roll up the flatbread
to make a perfect brunch burrito.

FULL ENGLISH GALETTE
SERVES 6–8

320g packet of ready-rolled
  puff pastry, thawed if frozen
400g can baked beans,
  drained slightly of sauce
50g Cheddar cheese,
  cut into 2.5cm cubes
8 rashers streaky bacon,
  roughly chopped
2 sausages, chopped into
  5mm-thick discs
Leaves from 4 sprigs
  fresh thyme
Salt and pepper
6 quail eggs

For the sauce (optional)
4 tbsp maple syrup
1 tsp yellow mustard seeds

Essential equipment
Baking sheet, lined
  with baking paper

I love a fry-up, that's no secret, but when you awake on your morning off, often the last thing you want to do is juggle kitchen timers to try to get every item ready in perfect harmony. With this method, though, not only is everything cooked in one go, but also you've got the added bonus of ready-rolled puff pastry, which frankly is a godsend at breakfast time. A 'galette' is a bake that's freeform and flat, and topped with ingredients.

1 Preheat the oven to 200°C/180°C fan/Gas 6.

2 Unroll the pastry on to the baking sheet, and score a 1cm-thick border around the edges. Place the drained baked beans on to the pastry, staying inside the 1cm border. Scatter over the cheese, bacon, sausages, thyme leaves and a pinch of salt and pepper. Slide into the oven and bake for 25 minutes.

3 After this time, remove the galette from the oven, then gently break the eggs, well spaced, on to the galette – try to keep the yolks plump and whole.

4 Return the galette to the oven and bake for a further 5–10 minutes, or until the egg whites have cooked through and the yolks are done to your liking.

5 To make the sauce, gently heat the maple syrup and mustard seeds in a small saucepan over a medium heat. When warm, drizzle over the galette.

GIANT BANANA BUTTERSCOTCH CHELSEA BUN
SERVES 10–12

For the dough
500g white bread flour
10g salt
15g golden caster sugar
10g fast-action yeast
200ml warm water
100ml milk
1 small egg, beaten
40g unsalted butter, softened

For the filling
100g unsalted butter,
  melted and cooled
100g dark muscovado sugar
200g dried ripe banana pieces
  (from a health food store)
150g small fudge pieces

For the glaze
50g golden caster sugar
50g water

For the butterscotch topping
50g light muscovado sugar
50g dark muscovado sugar
75g salted butter, in 1cm cubes
125ml double cream

Essential equipment
23cm/9-inch loose-bottomed
  cake tin, greased and lined
  with baking paper

Not only do I love this bake because of its size, but the flavours, too, are just out of this world. When this is on the breakfast table, it's definitely worth getting out of bed. If you can't get dried banana pieces from a health food store, use banana chips instead.

1 To make the dough, simply place the flour in a mixing bowl and stir through the salt and sugar, then the yeast. In a jug, beat together the water, milk and egg, add this to the dry ingredients, then add the butter in chunks. Stir the dough – elbow grease required – into a scraggy ball, then tip out on to the worktop and knead until you achieve a smooth, elastic dough – about 10–15 minutes. This is, admittedly, far easier in a freestanding electric mixer with dough hook attached – that will take about 7–10 minutes.

2 Place the dough in a floured or oiled bowl, and cover with a damp cloth and allow to rise until doubled in size. This could be between 1 and 3 hours, depending on the temperature of your room. Even longer if you live in a fridge-cold house.

3 When the dough has doubled in size, lightly flour the worktop and roll the dough into a rectangle of about 40 × 50cm. Paint over the melted butter, then sprinkle over the sugar, banana and fudge pieces. Slice the dough lengthways into strips 5cm wide. This will give you 8 long strips of dough. Take one of these strips and roll it into a tight spiral. Take another strip and wrap it around the first spiral to create a bigger one. Repeat until all the lengths of dough are used, and you have a giant spiral bun. Place it in the

GIANT BANANA BUTTERSCOTCH CHELSEA BUN
CONTINUED

prepared cake tin. It might be easier to do the first two spirals on the worktop, then continue the wrapping process in the tin.

4 Allow to rest for another 45–60 minutes, and preheat the oven to 200°C/180°C fan/Gas 6.

5 When the giant bun has rested, bake it for 25–30 minutes, or until golden on top.

6 Whilst the dough bakes, make the glaze and the butterscotch topping. For the glaze, put the sugar and water into a pan and bring to the boil. Boil for a minute then remove from the heat. For the butterscotch, put the ingredients into a medium pan and set over a high heat. Stirring constantly, allow the butter to melt and the sugar to dissolve into the cream and melted butter. Bring to the boil for just a minute, then remove from the heat.

7 When the giant bun comes out of the oven, paint the glaze all over the top. When it has cooled, spatter the butterscotch over the top.

MARMITE AND CHEDDAR SWIRL LOAF
SERVES 10–12

For the bread
250g strong white bread flour
5g salt
5g sugar
5g fast-action yeast
50ml milk
120ml warm water
30g butter, softened

For the filling
1–2 tsp Marmite, warmed
  slightly in the microwave
50–60g grated Cheddar cheese

Essential equipment
450g/1lb loaf tin
Rolling pin

Marmite offers a wonderful salty goodness to any meal, and I believe it is a good flavour in its own right, too. Swirled with cheese in a plain loaf, it makes for a tasty snack at brunch.

1 To make the bread, place all the ingredients in a bowl and squeeze together for a minute or so. Turn out on to the worktop and knead for 10 minutes or until smooth and elastic – or use a freestanding electric mixer fitted with a dough hook for 5–7 minutes. Place into a clean, oiled bowl, coat the dough in oil, then cover the bowl with cling film and leave to rise for 1 hour or until doubled in size.

2 When the dough has doubled in size, remove from the bowl on to the worktop. Roll the dough out into a rectangle that is the same width as your loaf tin's length. Using a pastry brush, paint the Marmite over the dough, then sprinkle over as much grated cheese as needed to cover the surface. Roll up tightly and place in the loaf tin. Allow to rise for 45 minutes.

3 Preheat the oven to 220°C/200°C fan/Gas 7.

4 When the loaf has risen, bake for 25–30 minutes, or until the base sounds hollow when the loaf is tipped out and gently tapped.

CLOUDY PURPLE CARROT CAKE

SERVES 8–10

4 eggs, separated
125g golden caster sugar
120g purple carrot,
   finely grated
Zest of 1 large lemon
1 tbsp vanilla bean paste
   or extract
150g ground almonds
10g cornflour

For the frosting
80g unsalted butter, softened
160g icing sugar
Zest of 1 lemon
250g full-fat cream cheese

Essential equipment
23cm/9-inch savarin mould,
   very well greased

Brunches, whilst leisurely, don't always have to be indulgently filling. This cloudy cake is so named thanks to its extremely light texture – somewhere between a sponge and angel food cake. The purple part is simply because I used purple carrots to make this after a trip to a farmers' market one day. The pale sponge flecked with shards of purple looks tempting, but if all you can get hold of are orange carrots, use those instead. This cake doesn't taste exactly like the bold, moist American carrot cakes, with their sweetness and chewiness. What it does have is a gentle resonance of the bolder carrot cakes while being lighter, earthier and absolutely gluten-free. The reason for the savarin mould is that it gives support; the light cake batter would sink in the middle if cooked in a regular round cake tin.

1 Preheat the oven to 200°C/180°C fan/Gas 6.

2 Place the egg whites in a mixing bowl and whisk until stiff peaks are achieved. Then, while continuing to whisk, add the sugar until you have a smooth, glossy meringue. You could also do this in a freestanding mixer with whisk attachment.

3 In another bowl, beat the egg yolks, most of the grated carrot, the zest and vanilla until well mixed, then scoop the meringue on to the yolk mixture along with the almonds and cornflour. Fold together – though do so vigorously: verging on a beat. When well amalgamated, pour into the well-greased savarin mould and bake for 20–25 minutes, or until lightly risen, golden, and a skewer inserted into the centre comes out relatively clean. Allow to cool in the tin, then carefully unmould on to a cake stand.

4 To make the frosting, place the butter into a mixing bowl and beat until very smooth, beat in the icing sugar and zest until fluffy, then carefully beat in the cream cheese – I always do this by hand with a wooden spoon because it's easy to split the cream cheese. When smooth, drape it over the cooled cake, scatter with the remaining grated carrot, and serve.

CHOCOLATE TEASER SOUFFLÉ
MAKES 4

2 tsp golden caster sugar
100g dark chocolate, roughly
  chopped – 60% is fine,
  don't go overly bitter
70g milk chocolate,
  roughly chopped
2 tbsp golden syrup
5 eggs, separated
1 tbsp mayonnaise
200g Maltesers,
  roughly bashed

For the sauce
100g milk chocolate
100ml double cream

100g Maltesers, bashed
  to fine pieces, to serve

Essential equipment
4 × 200ml ramekins, very
  well greased with butter
Baking sheet

This recipe is blissfully easy, but more importantly, it's decadently perfect for a lazy, indulgent brunch. The mayonnaise isn't a typing error – I use mayonnaise a lot when working with chocolate cakes I need to be gooey. The mayonnaise adds an egg-like texture, which helps create an unctuous inside because it doesn't coagulate like an egg.

1 Preheat the oven to 200°C/180°C fan/Gas 6.

2 Sprinkle the sugar into the greased ramekins and shake about so the sides and base are covered.

3 Place the chocolates and golden syrup into a heatproof bowl and set over a pan of barely simmering water. Allow the chocolate to slowly melt together with the syrup, stirring occasionally. Remove from the heat and allow to cool, but not set.

4 Meanwhile, put the egg whites into a mixing bowl and whisk until they are fluffy and stiff.

5 Beat the egg yolks into the chocolate along with the mayonnaise. Gently fold in the roughly bashed Maltesers, before very gently folding in the whisked whites – you want the mixture to be a smooth, even-toned batter, though of course with humps of Malteser.

6 Divide the mixture between the ramekins, cleaning the rim of each with your thumb. Set on to the baking sheet and bake for 10–12 minutes, or until beautifully risen. They may crack on top, but who cares – you're going to be diving in soon anyway.

7 To make the sauce, simply place the chocolate and cream in a heatproof bowl and set over a pan of simmering water. Stirring occasionally, allow the chocolate to melt into the cream until you have a smooth, glossy sauce.

8 To serve, tell the eater to take a spoonful out of the centre, then pour in some of glorious, warm sauce and top with crushed Maltesers.

PEANUT BUTTER, CHOCOLATE AND APRICOT BRIOCHE SWIRL
SERVES 10

For the brioche
250g white bread flour
5g salt
30g golden caster sugar
7g sachet fast-action yeast
150g egg (about 3)
20ml milk
125g unsalted butter, softened

For the filling
5 tbsp smooth peanut butter,
　beaten until very soft
4 tbsp apricot jam
100g milk chocolate, finely
　chopped
1 egg yolk beaten with
　1 tsp water and a pinch
　of salt, to glaze

Essential equipment
Freestanding electric mixer
　fitted with a dough hook
Baking tray, greased
Baking sheet lined with
　baking paper

This swirled brioche, filled with peanut butter, chocolate and apricot jam, makes brunch beautiful.

1 Place the flour, salt, sugar and yeast into the bowl of the freestanding mixer and mix together with a spoon or by hand. Beat the eggs with the milk, add to the bowl, and mix by hand before turning on the mixer so that the flour doesn't go everywhere. Knead on medium for 15 minutes, until the dough is stretchy.

2 Slowly add the butter piece by piece, mixing still on medium. It should take around 5 minutes to incorporate the butter. When done, allow the mixer to continue for about 5 minutes, until the dough is smooth, silky and very stretchy indeed. Place the dough in a greased baking tray, wrap tightly with cling film and put in the fridge overnight.

3 The next day, flour the worktop and roll out the dough to a rectangle of about 30 × 35cm. Spread with peanut butter, then dollop the jam over fairly evenly. Sprinkle over the chopped chocolate, then roll up into a tight spiral. Set this, seam side down, on to the baking sheet, and tuck the ends underneath to seal. Allow to rise for 1 hour, or until doubled in size.

4 Preheat the oven to 200°C/180°C fan/Gas 6.

5 Paint the surface of the loaf with the glaze and bake for 20–25 minutes. If after 15 minutes it looks dark, cover it with a sheet of foil. Allow to cool completely before slicing to serve.

AFTERNOON TEA AND PATISSERIE

When I walk past a London bakery window or look through the doors of a Parisian patisserie, I am always enchanted. I can't help but stare at the delicate creations, so evenly sized and beautifully arranged, gilded with gold leaf and dusted with sparkles. I only realized just how easy such patisserie is when I started my pastry diploma at Le Cordon Bleu in Bloomsbury. It's just baking with a French accent, and it really isn't impossible. Afternoon tea is undergoing a revival all across the country. There is something so greedily gratifying, but also elegant, about sitting down to a table adorned by a cake stand and picking at perfect bits and pieces. And besides, if I can eat more than one cake at any one time, I am a happy man.

ORANGE BRÛLÉE MILLE-FEUILLE
MAKES 6

320g packet of ready-rolled
  puff pastry (you could use
  homemade, but this is
  the perfect size)

For the brûlée topping
100g Demerara sugar

For the crème mousseline filling
1 quantity Crème Pâtissière
  (see page 252), cooled
  and set
Zest of 1 large orange
250g unsalted butter, softened

Essential equipment
2 large baking sheets and
  2 pieces of baking paper
Cook's blowtorch
Disposable piping bag fitted
  with 8mm nozzle
Confectioner's knife/sharp
  serrated knife

*The vanilla slices topped with fondant icing of my
childhood are a little too cloying now I'm an adult.
I much prefer this, with lashings of buttery crème
mousseline and the added crunch and darker sweetness
of a caramelized sugar topping (see overleaf). The
puff pastry for this mille-feuille is baked between two
baking sheets so you get the beautiful, buttery flakes
but without the added volume.*

1 Preheat the oven to 220°C/200°C fan/Gas 6.

2 Place a piece of baking paper on one of the baking
sheets and unroll the pastry on to it. Prick the pastry
well all over, then cover with the second piece of
baking paper, and the second baking sheet. If the
baking sheets have shallow sides, have the first sheet
upside down, then the second sheet the right way
up on top. Bake for 30–35 minutes, or until the
pastry is a deep golden brown.

3 When the pastry is baked, cut it lengthways with
a sharp knife into three equal strips and allow to cool.
When cool, sprinkle the Demerara sugar generously
over each strip, then, with the cook's blowtorch,
caramelize the sugar.

4 For the crème mousseline, put the crème pâtissière
into a mixing bowl and beat it to slacken it. I do
this in the freestanding electric mixer with whisk
attachment, but it could also be done in a mixing
bowl with a handheld electric whisk. Once the crème
pâtissière is loosened, beat in the zest, then slowly
add the butter bit by bit, beating constantly on
medium. It will take about 5 minutes to incorporate
all the butter, and the mixture should be thick.

5 Fill the piping bag with the crème mousseline and pipe it into neat rows along the length of one pastry strip. Place another pastry strip gently on top, then pipe the remaining mousseline on to this. Gently place the third and final strip of caramelized pastry on to the mousseline, then place the whole thing in the fridge to chill for at least two hours. (I build this up on a baking sheet so that I don't have to run a risk of breaking the whole thing in half, and I can easily pop it into the fridge.)

6 When the mille-feuille has chilled, the crème mousseline should have set quite firmly. With the sharp serrated knife and a gentle sawing motion, cut the whole thing in half crossways, then slice these two halves into three, to end with six neat mille-feuilles. If the mille-feuille was properly chilled, the mousseline should be firm enough to saw through without the whole thing collapsing in on itself, so long as you don't put too much pressure on when cutting.

CHOCO-BERRY FRAISIER CAKE
SERVES 8–10

For the genoise sponge

4 eggs

130g golden caster sugar

110g plain flour

20g cocoa powder

50g unsalted butter, melted
and cooled slightly

*For the blackcurrant crème
mousseline*

1 quantity Crème Pâtissière
(see page 252), cooled and set

2 tbsp crème de cassis liqueur

175g unsalted butter, cubed
and chilled slightly

75g white chocolate,
melted and cooled

INGREDIENTS CONTINUE OVERLEAF

Nothing signals the near end of a warm summer more than a fraisier. The classic French cake, literally meaning 'strawberry bush', is a patisserie shop classic, but it is also easy to make. I've adulterated the original, unashamedly adding blackberries and chocolate. Who could possibly resist such deliciousness?

1 Preheat the oven to 200°C/180°C fan/Gas 6.

2 Make the genoise sponge. This is best done in a freestanding electric mixer with whisk attachment, but if you don't have one then use a clean metal bowl and a handheld electric whisk. Place the eggs and sugar in the bowl and whisk until they about triple in volume and reach the ribbon stage – when you lift the whisk out of the bowl and draw a figure 8, the ribbon should sit proud on the surface for a few seconds. Sift together the flour and cocoa powder into a bowl, then gently sprinkle over the surface of the whisked eggs and sugar. With a flat spatula or large metal spoon, gently fold the flour into the eggs, ensuring that you scrape right to the bottom of the bowl too, but try not to deflate the mixture. When the flour is just about incorporated, pour the melted cooled butter down the side of the bowl and fold that in too. Gently pour this mixture into the cake ring and bake for about 25 minutes, or until a skewer inserted into the centre comes out clean. Remove from the oven, turn the cake ring upside down on a cooling rack, and allow to cool.

3 Make the blackcurrant crème mousseline following step 4 on page 58, but instead of orange zest, beat in the crème de cassis liqueur, then slowly add the

CHOCO-BERRY FRAISIER CAKE CONTINUED

For the soaking syrup
50g golden caster sugar
50g water
2 tbsp kirsch liqueur
½ tsp lemon juice

For the berry filling
400g strawberries (try to get smaller, even-sized ones)
150g blackberries (get the biggest ones you can)

For the topping
2 tbsp blackcurrant jam
50g natural marzipan
1 quantity freshly made Mirror Glaze (see page 251)
Gold leaf

Essential equipment
20cm/8-inch cake ring, 6cm/2½-inch deep, ungreased, on a baking sheet lined with baking paper
20cm/8-inch round cake card
Disposable piping bag fitted with 12mm plain nozzle

butter, then the white chocolate. Scrape into a bowl, cover with cling film and refrigerate.

4 Make the soaking syrup by heating together the sugar and water. Bring to the boil and allow to boil for a minute or two. Remove from the heat and stir in the kirsch and lemon juice.

5 Free the cake by scraping a knife around inside the cake ring and lifting it off. Slice the cake horizontally into two even slices, and set aside.

6 Clean the cake ring and place it on top of the cake card. Take the slice of cake that was the top and place this top side down into the cake ring. Soak it well with about half of the syrup, using a pastry brush to avoid completely drowning the cake. Take the most perfect strawberry and set it aside, then chop off the leafy ends of the rest, to create a flat bottom. Slice each strawberry in half down the length so that you can see the inside. Cut each blackberry in half this way too. Align the fruit against the sides of the tin: take a strawberry half and place it flat-bottom on to the layer of cake, cut middle pressed against the side. Place a blackberry half in the same way next to it, then alternate the fruits all the way around the circumference, gently squeezing them together so they stay in place (use the image on page 62 as a guide). Chop the remaining fruit roughly, and place it in a bowl.

7 Put the crème mousseline into the piping bag and pipe a spiral from the centre outwards on to the cake, ensuring you pipe in and amongst the berries at the edge – you won't need all of the mousseline at this point. Pile the remaining chopped fruits into the centre of the mousseline spiral, then pipe the remaining mousseline over the top. Smooth off with the back of a spoon. Take the second layer of cake, and place this cut-side down on to the mousseline, so that the original flat bottom of the cake is now the top.

Press down ever so gently, then soak that in the remaining syrup.

8 Paint the blackcurrant jam on to the surface of the cake, then roll out the marzipan to a circle the size of the cake – I use a little dusting of cornflour to prevent the marzipan sticking. Place this gently on top of the jam, so that it sticks to the cake. Place into the fridge while you make the mirror glaze finish, as described on page 251.

9 Allow the glaze to cool for just a minute so that it is still pourable. Pour enough glaze over the cake to cover the surface of the marzipan, but don't let it drip down the sides. Return the cake to the fridge and allow to cool for at least two hours.

10 When ready to serve, gently warm the cake ring by rubbing your hands around it – or carefully warm the cake ring with a cook's blowtorch, being careful not to get it too hot – then delicately lift up off the cake. Press gold leaf on to the perfect strawberry you reserved earlier, place on top, and serve. To retain the neat edges, cut with a sharp knife dipped in hot water.

MANGO & COCONUT MOUSSE CAKE
SERVES 12

When the summer months are in full flow and the sun is high in the sky, there is nothing more satiating than a tropical, fruity something. This is fairly tricky to master, but with patience and organization it can be achieved. The main thing to remember is to get the outer walls of the cake nice and tight, so they don't split open when you unmould it (see overleaf).

For the orange jelly insert
2 gelatine leaves
200ml orange juice
10g sugar

For the sponge
5 large eggs
125g golden caster sugar
125g flour

For the soaking syrup
75g golden caster sugar
50ml water
30ml coconut rum

For the mousse
4 gelatine leaves
75g golden caster sugar
75g water
800g mango pulp from
  a can
400ml double cream
50g desiccated coconut

1 Make the jelly insert: place the gelatine leaves, one by one, in a jug of cold water and allow to soak for 5 minutes. Heat the orange juice and sugar in a saucepan and bring to the boil, then squeeze the excess moisture out of the gelatine leaves and dissolve them in the hot orange juice. Pour this into the prepared 12.5cm cake tin and allow to cool, before transferring to the freezer to set completely.

2 Preheat the oven to 200°C/180°C fan/Gas 6.

3 Place the eggs and sugar in a large mixing bowl and whisk until very pale and fluffy. Using a handheld whisk, this will take about 10 minutes, or about 5–7 in a freestanding electric mixer with whisk attachment.

4 Sift the flour over the top of the whisked eggs and gently fold in using a spatula or large metal spoon. Pour at least two-fifths of this into the prepared Swiss roll tin, and divide the rest evenly between the 20cm cake tins. Bake all 3 for 8–10 minutes, or until the sponge springs back when gently touched. Allow to cool completely.

5 Make the soaking syrup by bringing the sugar and water to the boil, then remove from the heat and stir in the coconut rum.

6 When the cakes have cooled, peel the paper from them. Take the cake baked in the Swiss roll tin and slice it lengthways into 3 strips about 5cm wide.

Place the cake ring on the cake board, or directly on a cake stand, and place one of the two discs of cake in it. Dab on a little soaking syrup with a pastry brush.

7 Take one of the strips of cake and place it in the cake ring and against the side to create a wall. Put another strip next to it, and then, for the gap, slice off a piece from a third strip and pack that tightly between the other two, to create a continuous wall. Set to one side.

8 For the mousse, put the gelatine leaves, one by one, into a large bowl of cold water and allow to soak for 5 minutes. Boil the sugar and water, add the mango pulp, allow it all to come to a boil, then simmer until reduced by half. Remove from the heat. Remove the gelatine leaves from the soaking water and squeeze off the excess moisture, before adding them to the hot mango syrup. Mix well until dissolved. Allow to cool to blood temperature, before whipping the cream to soft, floppy peaks. Once whipped, gently pour the mango purée on to the whipped cream and fold it all together into a pale yellowish mixture. Fill the lined cake ring one-third full with the mousse.

9 Unmould the jelly disc and place it on top of the second disc of cake. Trim the cake so it is the same size as the jelly disc, then place this on the mousse layer, sponge-side down.

10 Pile more mousse into the cake ring so there is more than enough to fill it, then take a palette knife and gently drag the edges of the knife along the cake ring to smooth the mousse top. Sprinkle the desiccated coconut heavily over the surface.

11 Chill in the fridge overnight. To remove the cake from the ring, gently warm the sides with your hands, holding them in warm water beforehand if they are particularly cold, then gently lift the ring up and off.

Essential equipment
12.5cm/5-inch cake tin, greased and lined with cling film
30 × 20cm/12 × 8-inch Swiss roll tin, greased and lined with baking paper
2 loose-bottomed 20cm/8-inch cake tins, greased and the bases lined with baking paper
20cm/8-inch cake ring
20cm/8-inch cake board or cake stand

PRUNE AND ORANGE TARTLETS
MAKES 6

1 quantity Rich Sweet
  Shortcrust Pastry (see page
  248) or 500g shop-bought
  sweet shortcrust
180g dried prunes
150ml cola
2 shots of whisky

For the orange frangipane
120g salted butter, softened
120g golden caster sugar
2 eggs
120g ground almonds
Zest of 2 oranges
1 tsp orange blossom extract

To glaze
3 tbsp apricot jam
20ml water

Essential equipment
6-hole 10cm/4-inch mini
  pie tin
Disposable piping bag fitted
  with 10mm plain nozzle

These tartlets have that rugged, rustic look you'd expect, not from a French patisserie, but from a boulangerie. One with the longest of queues out of the door, where all the French go – the sign of a brilliant bakery. Though in spite of the rugged appearance, these will not at all look out of place on an afternoon tea table.

1 Preheat the oven to 200°C/180°C fan/Gas 6.

2 Roll out the pastry and use it to line the mini tart pan holes, then prick the base of each with a fork. Pop into the fridge to chill until needed.

3 Put the prunes and cola into a small saucepan and bring to the boil. Boil down, stirring, until the moisture is evaporated and you're left with soggy prunes. Stir in the whisky and allow to cool.

4 To make the orange frangipane, beat the butter and sugar together until pale and fluffy. This can be done by hand with an electric mixer, or in a freestanding mixer with paddle attachment. Beat in the eggs, almonds, zest and orange blossom extract, until you have a perfect batter.

5 Remove the lined tin from the fridge and divide the prune mixture between the tarts. Pipe the orange frangipane on top of the prunes so that it comes to just a couple of millimetres from the top edge of the pastry. Bake for 25–30 minutes, or until the frangipane is a luscious golden colour. Heat the jam in the water until it melts, then sieve and use to glaze the tartlets while they are still hot. Allow to cool in the tins to help crisp up the bases before serving.

PISTACHIO PRALINE MERINGUES

MAKES 18–20

6 egg whites
340g white caster sugar

For the praline
300g golden caster sugar
300g unsalted pistachios
  (shelled weight)
½ quantity Crème Pâtissière
  (see page 252)

Essential equipment
2 baking sheets lined
  with baking paper
Disposable piping bag
  fitted with 8mm nozzle
Disposable piping bag
  fitted with 10mm nozzle

What afternoon tea table would be complete without some little meringues? This recipe makes a powdery meringue, the kind you'd expect to get in a French bakery. Best served and eaten straightaway.

1 Preheat the oven to 140°C/120°C fan/Gas ½.

2 Set a saucepan of water over a high heat and bring to a gentle simmer. Put the egg whites in a heatproof mixing bowl with the caster sugar, place over the simmering water and whisk constantly until the mixture feels warm – not piping hot, but it should feel hot when a finger is dipped in. Then remove from the water bath and continue to whisk with either a handheld electric whisk or, better still, a freestanding mixer with whisk attachment. Whisk on full speed until the mixture is room temperature and very thick.

3 Pile the meringue into the piping bag fitted with an 8mm nozzle and pipe 18–20 nests on to the lined baking sheets. Start with a blob just a little bigger than a 2-pound coin, then pipe a circle around the edge, a circle on top of that, and a circle on top of that so you have a deep nest. The meringue, if done correctly, will be stiff enough to hold this shape.

4 Slide the meringues into the oven and at once reduce the heat to 120°C/100°C fan/Gas ¼. Bake for 25 minutes, then turn off the oven, open the door and allow the meringues to cool completely.

5 To make the praline, put a medium saucepan over a medium-high heat. Sprinkle in a third of the sugar and allow it to melt. Add another third, stir into the melted sugar and allow it to melt. Repeat with the remaining third, then allow the sugar to turn a golden amber. Add the pistachios – keep a handful back. Tip out on to baking paper and allow to cool completely, then snap into shards and blitz in a food processor until it turns into a gritty paste. Fold into the crème pâtissière, then scrape into the piping bag fitted with a 10mm nozzle and pipe into the meringue nests. Chop the reserved pistachios and scatter over the top.

APPLE AND LAVENDER SANDWICH TARTS

MAKES 10

Essential equipment
2 baking sheets lined
 with baking paper
Melon baller
7cm/2.5-inch circle
 cookie cutter
Deep-sided frying pan
Disposable piping bag
 fitted with 10mm nozzle

1 quantity Rough Puff Pastry
 (see page 246), or 500g
 shop-bought all-butter
 puff pastry

INGREDIENTS CONTINUE OVERLEAF

I first made this under pressure. It was 8 a.m. on a Friday morning and I was on the set of ITV's This Morning, *filming an 'ingredients reveal' for my blind bake. I had to choose two ingredients from a lucky dip, then create a dish to demonstrate live on air. I chose, thankfully, apples and lavender (the other options were peanut butter, chilli, filo pastry), then selected a big bottle of calvados from the store cupboard, took a good glug (or three) and cracked on. I would not have got through this without the help of Rashid Khalil and Julia Alger, who acted as sous-chefs on the day – many thanks to you both.*

1 Preheat the oven to 210°C/190°C fan/Gas 7.

2 Roll out half the pastry until it is just smaller than the baking sheet and about 4mm thick. Prick it all over with a fork, then place it on to a lined baking sheet. Top with the second piece of baking paper and then another baking sheet. This is to stop the pastry puffing up too much – you want the flakiness but not the volume. Bake for 25–30 minutes, or until a deep golden colour. As soon as the pastry comes out of the oven, cut out 10 discs with the cookie cutter. Allow these to cool completely. Repeat with the remaining half of pastry. (If you are generously supplied with baking sheets, you can do this all in a single batch.)

APPLE AND LAVENDER SANDWICH TARTS CONTINUED

For the poached 'applettes'
6 large eating apples (Cox or Braeburn are perfect)
1 lemon
500g golden caster sugar
500g water
1 tbsp dried lavender flowers
2 tbsp calvados

For the apple purée
Leftover apple from above (see step 3)
50g golden caster sugar

For the cream filling
225ml double cream
130g full-fat crème fraiche
1 tbsp vanilla bean paste or extract
1½ tbsp calvados
4 tbsp icing sugar

To finish
10 lavender flowers
Icing sugar, to dust

3 Peel the apples. Using the melon baller, scoop out at least 50 balls of apple. Put these straight into a mixing bowl with the juice of the lemon to prevent them from going brown and horrible. Don't throw away the used bits of apple; put them into a separate bowl with water and lemon juice.

4 To make a poaching liquid, put the sugar, water and lavender flowers into a deep-sided frying pan or large saucepan and bring to the boil. Reduce to a heavy simmer and add the apple balls. Simmer for 5 minutes until a sharp knife goes into an apple ball without any resistance. Remove from the heat and drain the apples, though do reserve the poaching syrup. Pour the calvados over the apple balls and leave in a small bowl until needed.

5 To make the apple purée, roughly chop the remaining chunks of apple – removing core and calyxes – and put into a small saucepan with the sugar and 6 tablespoons of the poaching liquid. Bring to the boil then reduce to a heavy simmer and allow the apples to cook down until mushy. Allow to cool.

6 To make the cream filling, simply whip the double cream to peaks that are just a little firmer than soft and floppy. Fold in the crème fraiche, vanilla, calvados and icing sugar and refrigerate until needed.

7 To assemble, take 10 of the pastry discs and place on a flat serving plate or tray. Fill the piping bag with the cream filling, then pipe a circle of filling on to each of the 10 pastry discs, just a few millimetres from the edge. Inside this circle of filling, dot 5 balls of poached apple, evenly spaced. In the centre of the apples, place a scant teaspoon of the apple purée. Squeeze some of the cream over the apple purée so that it sneaks in between the apples and joins the first circle of filling. Top with another disc of puff pastry. You should have 10 perfect tarts. Top each one with a small sprig of lavender flowers, and a heavy dusting of icing sugar.

RASPBERRY & PISTACHIO GENOISE SLICES MAKES 8

Essential equipment
20cm/8-inch square cake
  tin, greased and fully lined
  with baking paper
Extra baking paper
Disposable piping bag fitted
  with 10mm plain nozzle
Sharp serrated knife, such
  as a confectioner's knife

For the genoise
5 eggs
165g golden caster sugar
Zest of 1 lemon
165g plain flour
60g unsalted butter, melted
  and cooled

For the soaking syrup
60g golden caster sugar
60ml water
4 tbsp eau de vie framboise
  (a raspberry liqueur),
  or crème de cassis if easier
  to find

INGREDIENTS CONTINUE OVERLEAF

This is a fairly technical bake, but don't let that put you off, because its taste is a summer's day in Paris. The recipe calls for pistachio paste – this can easily be bought online, but if you have a food processor, why not have a go at the recipe on page 249.

1 Preheat the oven to 200°C/180°C fan/Gas 6.

2 To make the genoise, make sure the tin is greased and lined all over – sorry to harp on, but it's vital.

3 Put the eggs, sugar and zest into a heatproof mixing bowl and set over a pan of barely simmering water. Whisk together with an electric handheld mixer until the mixture feels slightly warm, then remove from the heat and continue whisking until the eggs have tripled in volume and you have achieved the ribbon stage – when you lift the whisk out of the mixture, the batter falls from the whisk and sits proud on the surface for at least 4 seconds. If you have a freestanding electric mixer, simply do it in that on full speed – much quicker, and no need for the warm water. Sift the flour over the surface and very gently fold in, ensuring no clumps lurk at the bottom. When the flour is just about folded in, pour the melted, cooled butter down the side of the bowl into the mixture and fold that in too.

4 Carefully – and I mean carefully – pour the batter into the prepared cake tin, and bake for 20–25 minutes, or until a skewer inserted into the centre comes out clean. Remove from the oven and allow to cool in the tin until completely cold.

5 For the syrup, mix the sugar and water together and bring to the boil on a high heat. Allow to bubble for 2 minutes, then remove from the heat and allow to cool, before stirring in the liqueur.

RASPBERRY AND PISTACHIO GENOISE SLICES CONTINUED

For the crème mousseline filling
1 quantity Crème Pâtissière
   (see page 252), cooled
250g unsalted butter, softened
100g Pistachio Paste
   (see page 249)
170g raspberries
   (as firm as possible)

To decorate
12 plump raspberries
Icing sugar

6 To make the crème mousseline filling, take the cooled crème pâtissière and scoop it into a mixing bowl – or the bowl of a freestanding electric mixer fitted with whisk attachment. Whisk it vigorously until fairly smooth, then slowly start to add the butter in small lumps, whisking well after each addition until the butter is well incorporated – make sure you scrape the mixture off the side of the bowl with a spatula if it starts to stick. When the butter is all added, crumble in the pistachio paste and continue whisking on full for a minute or so until it is well incorporated. Scoop this pistachio mousseline into the piping bag.

7 When the cake is cold, remove it from the tin and carefully slice off any domed top – get it as level as possible. Then, with a straight eye and a sharp serrated knife, slice the cake horizontally in half as evenly as possible.

8 Re-grease and line the tin with baking paper, leaving plenty of baking paper overhanging so that you can easily lift out the finished cake, then place the top half of the cake – cut-side up – into the tin. Soak that with a generous amount of the soaking syrup, press the cake down gently so that it fills the base of the cake tin, then pipe even lines of mousseline to just cover the top. Scatter the raspberries on top, then pipe the remaining mousseline over them. Soak the cut side of the other cake half (this should have originally been the bottom half, so that the flat base can now become the top) and place that – cut-side down – on to the mousseline. Gently press the cake down to even everything out, then wrap well with cling film (still in the cake tin) and refrigerate for at least 3 hours, preferably overnight.

9 When the cake has cooled, lift it out of the tin, trim the edges with a sharp serrated knife to neaten, and then cut into 8 equal slices. Top each slice with a raspberry, and a generous dusting of icing sugar.

ORANGE & CARDAMOM OPERA

SERVES 8

Essential equipment

Two 20 × 30cm/8 × 12-inch
   Swiss roll tins, greased and
   fully lined with baking paper
20cm/8-inch square cake board
   (optional but handy)

For the biscuit sponge

4 eggs
100g ground pistachios
50g ground almonds, grind
   your own in a food processor
   if necessary
150g icing sugar
45g flour
5 egg whites
25g sugar
40g unsalted butter, melted

For the ganache

100ml milk
8 cardamom pods, bruised
200g dark chocolate,
   roughly chopped
20g unsalted butter, softened

INGREDIENTS CONTINUE OVERLEAF

Like a true opera, with its eye-watering emotion and devilishly dramatic storyline, the opera cake is a thing of sheer beauty. The defined layers are impressive on the eye, whilst the gentle warmth of cardamom, and the age-old unity of chocolate and orange, are heavenly on the tongue. This is absolutely perfect for afternoon tea parties with friends and family, or even if you just fancy a bit of a challenge.

1 Preheat the oven to 200°C/180°C fan/Gas 6.

2 Place the eggs, ground pistachios, ground almonds, icing sugar and flour into a mixing bowl and beat together until well combined and smooth. It is best to do this in a freestanding electric mixer with whisk attachment, or at least using an electric handheld mixer. In another bowl, whisk the egg whites to stiff peaks, then add the sugar in three incorporations, whisking well after each addition, until the sugar is dissolved. Scoop this meringue on top of the egg and nut mixture, and pour on the melted butter. Gently fold together until just incorporated, trying not to expel too much air. The mixture should be fairly runny.

3 Divide the mixture between the prepared tins and smooth the surfaces. Bake for 12–15 minutes, or until lightly golden in colour and when pressed lightly the sponge springs back. Remove from the oven and allow to cool completely before removing from the tins, trying not to break any sponge.

4 As the sponges bake, make the ganache. Place the milk in a saucepan with the bruised cardamom pods

ORANGE AND CARDAMOM OPERA CONTINUED

For the soaking syrup
60g sugar
60ml water
4 cardamom pods, bruised
100ml orange juice

For the orange buttercream
75g unsalted butter, softened
Zest from 1 large orange
150g icing sugar
1 tsp fresh orange juice

To decorate
1 quantity Mirror Glaze
  (see page 251)
Gold leaf to decorate

and set over a high heat. When the mixture begins to steam, remove from the heat and allow the cardamom to infuse into the milk for about 10 minutes. Remove the cardamom pods and reheat the milk on medium-high until bubbles just begin to form around the edges. Place the chopped chocolate in a heatproof bowl and pour the hot milk over it. Allow the milk to heat the chocolate for about 30 seconds, then use a whisk to blend together to a smooth, glossy ganache. Whisk in the butter until it is well incorporated, then pour on to a large plate and set aside to cool.

5 To make the soaking syrup, place the sugar, water and bruised cardamom pods in a saucepan and set over a high heat. Bring to the boil, allow to boil for about 3 minutes, then turn off the heat and leave to cool slightly. Stir in the orange juice and allow to infuse.

6 To make the buttercream, place the butter and zest in a bowl and whisk until pale and smooth, then sift in the icing sugar and add the orange juice. Beat slowly at first until the butter and icing sugar come together, then whisk vigorously for at least 5 minutes – this is where you need a freestanding mixer with whisk attachment or at least a handheld electric whisk. The buttercream should become very pale and light.

7 To assemble, cut the two sponges into two pieces: you need from each a square of 20 × 20cm, and a piece of 10 × 20cm (so in total two 20cm squares and two 10 × 20cm rectangles). Place one of the 20 × 20cm squares on a board and soak it well with some of the syrup using a pastry brush. Then take the ganache and test if it is ready: you should be able to spread it into a mound, which should hold its shape. Spread two-thirds of the ganache on to this first layer – don't worry if it oozes down the side as you will trim it anyway. Chill for a few minutes.

8 Place the two rectanglar pieces of sponge on the ganache and soak well with some syrup, then take the buttercream and gently spread that on to the sponges, again not worrying if some dribbles down the side. Chill for a few more minutes.

9 Take the final square of sponge and soak it well with syrup then place soaked-side-down on to the buttercream. Spread the remaining ganache evenly over the top of the cake, and place in the fridge, or ideally the freezer, for a good 20 minutes.

10 Make the mirror glaze as described on page 251, or, if you made it earlier and it has set, place it in a microwave and heat on medium for 30-second bursts until glossy and runny again. Pour this over the chilled cake, ensuring the glaze sets evenly on top – it doesn't need to dribble down the sides, but if it does, again don't worry. Put back into the fridge for a good 20 minutes to set.

11 When the mirror glaze has set, take a very sharp knife, dip it in a large jug of boiling water, then dry quickly on a cloth. Slice a tiny amount from each edge – just 5mm if you can. This will create nice, defined layers. Then, repeating the knife-heating technique, cut the opera into 4 equal squares, and cut each square in half into equal slices. You will have 8 slices. Decorate with as much – or as little, if you have the self-restraint I clearly lack – as you like of gold leaf.

CHOCA-COLA MACARONS
MAKES 24

100g ground almonds
100g icing sugar
2 egg whites
140g golden caster sugar
70ml water
Brown food colouring

To slacken
15g egg white

For the filling
150g plain chocolate,
  roughly chopped
75ml cola

For the topping
2 tbsp light brown soft sugar
½ tsp edible citric acid – ask
  the pharmacist to ensure
  it is edible!

Essential equipment
Sugar or digital thermometer
2 baking sheets lined with
  silicone mats (or baking
  paper if that's all you can get)
Disposable piping bags, one
  fitted with 8mm nozzle

I love these so much. The sharp fizz of the citric acid and sugar coupled with the chocolaty cola filling is moreish. I first had these at a Chinese restaurant in Soho, and fell in love with them. This recipe calls for Italian meringue, which enables immediate baking of the macaron shells, rather than having to allow the 'crust' to form as one would with French macarons.

1 Preheat the oven to 180°C/160°C fan/Gas 4.

2 Place the almonds and icing sugar in a food processor and blitz to a very fine powder. Sift this into a bowl – then, if you're as fussy as I am, sift it again.

3 Place the egg whites in the heatproof mixing bowl of a freestanding electric mixer with whisk attachment. (You could also do this using a handheld electric whisk.) Beat the egg whites until they are at soft peak stage (see page 11), then stop mixing.

4 Place the sugar and water in a medium saucepan over a medium-high heat, and clip the sugar thermometer in place. If your thermometer doesn't have a clip, simply hold it. Do not stir the mixture at any point, just leave it to boil and bubble away. When the thermometer reads 118°C or 'softball stage' – after about 5 minutes – remove the pan from the heat immediately, being careful because the mixture is very hot. Turn the mixer for the egg whites back on to medium speed and continue mixing as you gently pour the sugar syrup down the side of the bowl. Add the brown colouring and continue whisking on high until the meringue has cooled to room temperature. This will take about 6 or 7 minutes.

5 Gently scoop the meringue on top of the almond-sugar mix and, using a spatula, fold together until smooth, then fold in the 15g egg white until the mixture drops from a spoon like magma.

6 Scrape this into the piping bag and pipe blobs about the size of a 10p piece on to the baking sheet. Space them well apart so they can spread. The best way to pipe them is to hold the piping bag at an angle of just under 90 degrees from the sheet, and hold it fairly close so the blob doesn't form ridges. Once you have piped all the blobs – about 48 in total – gently tap the baking sheets on to the worktop to spread the macarons out evenly.

7 Place the baking sheets in the oven and bake for 4 minutes. After 4 minutes, quickly open and close the door a few times to get rid of any harsh burn or humidity, then bake for a further 4 minutes. Repeat the opening and closing, then bake for a final 4 minutes – they should be baked for 12 minutes with two door-openings in between. Make sure the macarons are sufficiently baked – gently tap one on the rim, and if it trembles only very slightly, they are ready. If not, give it a minute or two more. Remove from the oven, slide the silicone mat or baking paper on to the worktop and allow the shells to cool.

8 For the filling, place the chocolate in a heatproof bowl. Put the cola into a small saucepan and heat on high until it boils. Remove from the heat, allow to cool for about 2 minutes, then pour it over the chopped chocolate. Stir together with a whisk until you have a smooth, glossy ganache, then spread it on to a plate to cool and thicken.

9 When the ganache is thick like chocolate spread, scrape it into another piping bag, snip a little off the end of the bag and pipe a blob on to the flat side of half the shells, then sandwich the empty shells on top.

10 In a small bowl, mix together the sugar and citric acid, then sprinkle a little on top of each macaron. The sooner these are served, the fizzier the effect.

ARABIAN NIGHTS TART SERVES 8–10

1 quantity Rich Sweet
   Shortcrust Pastry
   (see page 248)
1 quantity Cardamom Crème
   Pâtissière (see page 252)
1 egg white, beaten, to glaze

*For the pistachio and
   orange frangipane*
100g unsalted pistachios
30g ground almonds
1 tbsp plain flour
120g salted butter, cubed
100g golden caster sugar
2 eggs

For the topping
160g blueberries
200g seedless white grapes,
   cut in half widthways
Seeds of 1 large pomegranate
5 tbsp apricot jam
2–3 tbsp water
Pistachios and almond flakes,
   to decorate

Essential equipment
25cm/10-inch loose-bottomed
   tart or flan tin
Baking sheet
Disposable piping bag fitted
   with 10mm nozzle

I'm obsessed with spice. When I cook savoury suppers there has to be cardamom or sumac in there. This tart has the provocative hint of cardamom in the crème pâtissière and a divine pistachio frangipane. As you can see, it is a joy to behold, and not overly sweet. If you can find golden raspberries for the inner circle, as we used here, then snap them up; otherwise use grapes.

1 Roll out the pastry to about 5mm thick and use it to line the tin. Refrigerate for 30 minutes.

2 Preheat the oven to 200°C/180°C fan/Gas 6 and place a baking sheet in there to heat up.

3 To make the frangipane, grind together the pistachios, almonds and flour in a food processor, then add the remaining ingredients and grind to a thick batter. Put into the piping bag and pipe into the base of the pastry case in concentric circles until the base is full, then bake in the oven, on the preheated baking sheet, for 30–35 minutes, or until the frangipane is baked through and the pastry case is crisp. Remove from the oven and allow to cool.

4 When the tart is cool, spread the crème pâtissière on top of the frangipane and even out.

5 To finish the tart with its fruity top, starting on the outside of the tart make a circle out of blueberries – if you're a perfectionist, try to select blueberries of roughly the same size. Then do a circle of white grape halves, then a thick circle of pomegranate seeds. Repeat until you have perfect concentric circles.

6 To finish, place the apricot jam into a small saucepan with the water and heat until it boils. Sieve into a bowl, then paint generously over the fruit top. Finish with a scattering of almond flakes and pistachios.

CHOCOLATE LUSTRE CAKE
SERVES 12–14

250ml water
100g dark chocolate chips
250g salted butter
100g cocoa powder
200g light brown soft sugar
200g golden caster sugar
140g Greek yoghurt
2 eggs
1 tbsp vanilla bean paste
   or extract
275g plain flour
2 tsp bicarbonate of soda

*For the chocolate ganache
   crumb coat*
300ml double cream
200g dark chocolate chips
200g milk chocolate chips

To decorate
1 quantity freshly made
   Mirror Glaze (see page 251)
Edible gold shimmer spray
1 tsp edible gold lustre

Essential equipment
23cm/9-inch springform
   round cake tin, greased and
   lined with baking paper
23cm/9-inch round cake card
Icing turntable (if possible)
Crank-handled palette knife
Wire rack with baking paper
   underneath to catch the drips

This cake was inspired by one I saw in a shop window in Le Marais, Paris. The shop itself looked a little down-at-heel, but in the window sat this awe-inspiring cake. I just had to stand and stare … until dragged away by bored partner. This is the ultimate in chocolate cakes. Its strong cocoa flavour is simply beautiful – only a small slice is required.

1 Preheat the oven to 170°C/150°C fan/Gas 3.

2 Place the water, chocolate chips and butter in a heatproof bowl and set over a saucepan of just simmering water. Allow to warm through until both the chocolate and butter have melted into the water. Remove from the heat and allow to cool, before adding the cocoa powder, sugars and yoghurt. Beat until well incorporated, then add the eggs and vanilla, before sifting over the flour and bicarb and folding those in too.

3 Pour the batter into the prepared cake tin, and bake for 45 minutes to an hour, or until a skewer inserted into the centre of the cake comes out clean. Allow to cool in the tin until completely cold.

4 To make the chocolate ganache crumb coat, place the cream in a small saucepan and set over medium heat. Place the chocolate chips in a heatproof bowl. When the cream starts to bubble around the edges, pour over the chocolate chips and allow to warm them for a minute, then with a whisk beat to a smooth, glossy ganache. Allow this to cool – on a tray is best – until it is the consistency of a chocolate spread.

5 If the cake has domed slightly in the middle, trim it so that it is perfectly flat-topped. Place on to the cake card, and on to an icing turntable if possible. Now

CHOCOLATE LUSTRE CAKE
CONTINUED

'mask' the cake (see page 12). Using the crank-handled palette knife, apply the ganache, spreading it delicately on top of the cake and around the sides. Get it as straight and smooth as possible – the more perfect this layer, the better the mirror glaze will look. I first concentrate on getting the top well covered, and then I manipulate and gently spread the ganache around the sides. Finish it off by neatening the corner where the top meets the sides, and chill for 15 minutes.

6 Meanwhile, make the mirror glaze as described on page 251. Pass the glaze through a sieve into a cold bowl and allow to cool for a minute – it still needs to be warm so that it is runny, rather than cooled and set.

7 To finish the cake off, place it – still on the cake card – on to the wire rack. Pour the glaze over the masked cake, easing it down the sides while trying not to disturb the natural flow. To paint the gold strip, in a small ramekin spray plenty of the shimmer spray so that it pools in the bottom, then add the lustre. Mix together, then dip a paintbrush in and gently drag in a line across a segment of the glazed cake (see the image on page 88). If the mirror glaze needs a little retouching, don't spread it with a palette knife, simply waft a hairdryer over it, on warm but medium speed, and this should melt the mirror glaze and reset it.

8 Allow the glaze to set for an hour or two before serving.

CRAB & AVOCADO ÉCLAIRS
MAKES 10

½ quantity Choux Pastry
  (see page 246)
1 egg yolk beaten with
  1 tsp water, to glaze

For the filling
150g full-fat cream cheese
1 ripe avocado
120g white crab meat
2 tbsp freshly chopped chives
2 tbsp freshly chopped dill
1 tbsp horseradish sauce
½ tsp sea salt flakes
1 tsp cracked black pepper
Zest and juice of 1 lime

Essential equipment
Baking sheet greased very
  lightly with butter
Disposable piping bag fitted
  with large star nozzle
Disposable piping bag fitted
  with 10mm plain nozzle

An afternoon tea table, whilst mainly scattered with sweet goods, should always have at least one savoury offering. These savoury éclairs not only fit in perfectly with their choux pastry shells, but their light and balanced filling is very welcome on the table. The filling is just as good slathered over slices of sourdough or rye bread and served with a little slice of lemon or lime.

1 Preheat the oven to 220°C/200°C fan/Gas 7.

2 Make 10cm-long marks on the baking sheet. The most effective way to do this is to cut a piece of card to 10cm. Dip this in flour and then tap it on the greased baking sheet to make a line. Repeat this dipping and tapping until you have 10 lines, evenly spaced across the baking sheet. Chill the baking sheet in the fridge.

3 Make the choux pastry according to the method on page 246, then load it into the piping bag fitted with the large star nozzle. Pipe 10 even lines of choux, following the marks on the baking sheet – apply an even pressure and let the choux fall gently. Don't drag the pastry as it falls, just let it drop naturally and move your piping bag with it. Once you have 10 lines of choux, very carefully glaze each with the egg yolk and water glaze using a pastry brush. Bake the éclairs for 20–25 minutes, or until a deep golden colour and crispy. Allow to cool completely, and then slice each in half.

4 To make the filling, beat the cream cheese to soften, then finely chop the avocado, squidge it with a potato masher or fork and beat it into the cream cheese – do this by hand, otherwise the cream cheese could easily over-soften. Fold in the crab meat, chives, dill and horseradish, then add the salt, pepper, lime zest and juice, and mix until just incorporated – over-mixing could cause the lime juice to split the cream cheese.

5 Scrape the mixture into the piping bag with the plain nozzle. Fill each bottom half of éclair with the mixture, then pop on the top half.

FAMILY BAKES

It seems there are some bakes that are perfect for grown-up social occasions, while others – such as these – best suit the classic family kitchen. My love of baking derives almost entirely from time spent with my family in the kitchen, so these recipes are very close to my heart. They are family-oriented and child-friendly, with a hint of nostalgia for childhood past, but they are not boringly traditional. I've gone for bakes that children will enjoy for their comforting sweetness, while adults can appreciate them for their originality of flavour or method or their playfulness.

SHERBET LEMON CAKE
SERVES 8–10

For the candied lemon topping
2 lemons
600ml water (in batches
    of 200ml)
100g sugar
100ml water
75g golden caster sugar

For the cake
Zest of 3 lemons
4 eggs
225g golden caster sugar
225g butter, very soft
225g self-raising flour
1 tsp baking powder

For the filling
400ml whipping cream
500g mascarpone cheese
300g icing sugar
Zest of 2 lemons
1 tbsp lemon juice
2 packets of lemon Dip Dabs
    (sherbet only)

Icing sugar, to dust

Essential equipment
Two 20cm/8-inch loose-
    bottomed round cake tins,
    greased and lined with
    baking paper
Cake stand at least 20cm/
    8 inches across
Disposable piping bag fitted
    with 12mm nozzle

*The word 'sherbet' evokes memories of youth,
but, ironically, I disliked sherbet as a child –
I was a kid who needed a more toothsome, chewy
sort of jelly sweet. This cake is perfect for baking
with children, because the cake batter uses a 'one
mix' method, so there is no need to go through the
stages of making a cake, which can sometimes tire
fickle little kids. And though it's a simple cake to
make, with a simple filling, the presentation takes
it up a notch. This cake is a nod to all things youthful,
but it is also absolutely acceptable at a sophisticated,
child-free gathering.*

1 For the lemon topping, use a potato peeler to
pare thick strips of peel from the lemons – if you
get any white pith, scrape it off with a knife. Chop
the lemon peel into thin matchsticks, then place in
a small saucepan with 200ml water. Bring to the boil,
then drain the water, place the lemon zest back into
the pan with another 200ml water and repeat. Drain
again then repeat – you should bring the lemon zest
to the boil 3 times in total. Set the drained lemon zest
matchsticks aside. Place the 100g sugar and 100ml
water in the saucepan and bring to the boil until the
sugar is dissolved, then return the lemon zest and
allow to poach for about 5 minutes. Drain. Place
the 75g caster sugar in a bowl and add the lemon
matchsticks. Toss in the sugar then arrange on a
baking sheet and allow to dry out for a few hours
(overnight is better).

2 Preheat the oven to 180°C/160°C fan/Gas 4.

3 Place the ingredients for the cake into a mixing
bowl and beat together until well incorporated and
smooth. If you have a freestanding electric mixer,

SHERBET LEMON CAKE
CONTINUED

use the paddle attachment. Divide the batter between the two prepared tins, and bake for 20–25 minutes, or until golden brown and a skewer inserted into the centre comes out clean. Remove from the oven and allow to cool slightly, before removing from the tins and turning on to a cooling rack until completely cold.

4 Meanwhile, make the filling by whipping the cream to very soft floppy peaks. Fold this into the mascarpone along with the sifted icing sugar and lemon zest until smooth. Then quickly beat in the lemon juice – though don't overbeat, as you don't want the mixture to split.

5 When the cake is cooled, and the candied lemon is dry, slice each cake in half horizontally so that you have four layers. Place one on the cake stand. Fill the piping bag with the filling and pipe little blobs around the edge of the cake, then a spiral of filling in the centre. Sprinkle over a third of the sherbet, then top with another slice of cake. Repeat this until you have four layers of cake and three layers of cream and sherbet. Sift a layer of icing sugar over the top, then scatter over the candied lemon matchsticks.

TWO-TONED MADELEINES
MAKES 16

100g golden caster sugar
2 eggs
1 tsp vanilla bean paste
    or extract
100g plain flour
½ tsp baking powder
100g unsalted butter, melted
2 food colours of your choice
Icing sugar, to dust

Essential equipment
Madeleine tin (16-hole
    preferably, but 12 suffices),
    greased and lightly floured
Piping bag fitted with
    10mm nozzle

Whenever I bake for my nephews, they can never truly decide on just one flavour, and their multiple choices often seem contradictory – such as beef and chocolate. These little two-toned cakes are a great treat for undecided children, something to admire and devour.

1 Place the sugar, eggs and vanilla into a mixing bowl and beat with a handheld electric whisk until much lighter in colour and tripled in volume. (A freestanding electric mixer with whisk attachment, if you have one, would make the job easier.) Then sift the flour and baking powder over the entire surface of the mixture, and fold in with a large spatula or metal spoon until the flour is just incorporated with no clumps. Gently pour the melted, cooled butter down the side of the bowl, and fold that in too.

2 Divide the mixture evenly between two bowls, add a little colour to each and fold in until you achieve the desired effect. Place the bowls in the fridge and allow the batter to chill and firm up for about an hour.

3 Preheat the oven to 200°C/180°C fan/Gas 6.

4 When the mixture is nicely firm, scrape one colour into one side of the piping bag, then scrape the second colour into the other side of the piping bag. Twist the end of the bag so the coloured batters move down to the nozzle in unison, then fill each madeleine mould with a fat sausage of dual-toned batter. It will spread and rise in the oven, so don't fill the moulds completely – just one fat sausage will do.

5 Bake for 8–10 minutes, or until the madeleines have puffed up, and spring back when gently prodded. Unmould and dust with plenty of icing sugar.

PEANUT BUTTER AND JELLY CUPCAKES
MAKES 12

60g smooth peanut butter
100g butter, softened,
   or baking spread
125g golden caster sugar
75g seedless raspberry jam
2 eggs
150g plain flour
1 tsp baking powder

For the topping
80g butter, softened
45g smooth peanut butter
200g icing sugar
6 tsp seedless raspberry jam

Essential equipment
12-hole deep muffin tray,
   lined with muffin cases
Disposable piping bag

What a classic combination for kids! I remember as a little boy I used to nag and nag my mum to send me to school with peanut butter and jam sandwiches. She rarely did, but on the odd occasion that I did open my lunchbox and peered in to find them, I would gobble them up quickly before Kay, the naughty girl, managed to pinch them. The cake batter uses a simple 'one-mix' method, so this is perfect for making with kids.

1 Preheat the oven to 190°C/170°C fan/Gas 5.

2 To make the cake batter, simply place all the ingredients in a bowl and mix together. You can use a freestanding electric mixer with paddle attachment, or a wooden spoon – but then a little elbow grease is required. When well blended, divide the mixture between the muffin cases and bake for 20–22 minutes, or until a skewer inserted into the centre comes out clean. Remove from the oven and allow to cool completely.

3 To make the frosting, place the butter and peanut butter in a mixing bowl and beat until very smooth. Add the icing sugar and stir gently to avoid creating a sweet, dusty cloud. When the sugar is mixed in, whisk well to incorporate some air – I do this in a freestanding electric mixer with whisk attachment, but an electric handheld whisk would do. Whisk for at least 5 minutes.

4 To finish the cupcakes, place the frosting in the piping bag and snip off the end to create a hole of about 1cm in diameter. Pipe two concentric circles around the edge of the cupcakes, leaving a hole in the middle. Into that hole on each cupcake, gently spoon half a teaspoon of the jam – to make it easier to spoon, beat the jam in a cup before using.

AUSSIE CRUNCH
SERVES 12

250g unsalted butter
175g golden caster sugar
125g desiccated coconut
100g cornflakes
12g cocoa powder
200g self-raising flour
100g milk chocolate

Essential equipment
20cm/8-inch square or
  23cm/9-inch round cake
  tin, greased and lined
  with baking paper

This recipe is from my lovely friend Alex Holt, who first made this for me a while ago. Why it is called Aussie Crunch when it comes from Bolton is a mystery, but it really is delicious, and so simple that it is perfect for making with kids. That said, Alex makes this for our grown-up parties too, and it is usually the first thing to fly from the dessert table.

1 Preheat the oven to 200°C/180°C fan/Gas 6.

2 Place the butter and sugar in a medium saucepan and set over medium heat. Allow the butter to melt and the sugar to dissolve.

3 Meanwhile, place the coconut and cornflakes into a mixing bowl and toss together, then sift in the cocoa and flour and toss again. Pour the melted butter and sugar over the dry ingredients, then press into the cake tin and bake for 20 minutes.

4 Whilst the crunch is still hot, break the chocolate over the top of it and allow it to melt.

5 Allow to cool before removing from the tin and gobbling up.

GIANT JAM TART

SERVES 10–12

320g packet of all-butter,
    ready-rolled puff pastry
150g raspberries
100g blueberries
175g golden caster sugar
1 egg, beaten with a tiny
    pinch of salt, to glaze

Essential equipment
Baking sheet lined with
    baking paper
Lattice cutter

With a little attempt at making a childhood classic that bit more sophisticated by adding a glazed lattice, this giant jam tart is an absolute pleasure to make and eat. What's more, it's laughably simple.

1 Preheat the oven to 200°C/180°C fan/Gas 6.

2 Unroll the pastry and cut off one-fifth of it, along the shortest side. Place the two pieces of pastry back in the fridge until required.

3 Make the jam by placing the raspberries, blueberries and sugar in a saucepan. Bring to the boil, then reduce to a simmer for 10–15 minutes, or until the jam is thick – take out a spoonful, let it cool slightly, squeeze it between your forefinger and thumb, then open and close your fingers and there should be a faint thread of jam.

4 Spread the jam over the surface of the larger piece of pastry, but leave a margin of about 1cm around the edge, and glaze that with a touch of beaten egg. With the lattice cutter, cut the remaining one-fifth of pastry into a lattice, spread the strands delicately apart, then place over the tart and seal it on to the egg-painted edges of the base pastry. Carefully glaze the lattice with a little egg, then bake for 20–25 minutes, or until puffed up around the edges, a glorious golden colour, and the jam is thick and sweet.

ROLO MERINGUE KISSES
MAKES 20

2 packs Rolos
3 egg whites
170g golden caster sugar

Essential equipment
Re-sealable sandwich bag
Disposable piping bag
  with 12mm nozzle
Baking sheet lined with
  baking paper

Meringue is so easy to make, and whilst it is delicious on its own, it's even better with the hidden surprise of melted chocolate and toffee centres. These are great for kids to do; the meringue is fairly easy, and adding a Rolo is just, well, child's play. These are scrumptious on their own, but you could always glue them together with chocolate ganache for an even more indulgent treat.

1 The day before making these, empty the Rolos into a re-sealable sandwich bag and place into the freezer.

2 On the day of making, preheat the oven to 140°C/120°C fan/Gas 1. To make the meringue, beat the egg white to medium-stiff peaks. This is best done in a freestanding electric mixer with whisk attachment. With the beater still running, slowly add the sugar a tablespoon at a time, whisking well until the sugar has dissolved into the whites and you have a stiff, glossy meringue.

3 Scoop the meringue into the piping bag and pipe 20 blobs, about the size of a 2-pound coin, on to the baking sheet. Place a frozen Rolo into the centre of each blob, then top each Rolo with a generous peak of meringue so that it is entirely covered. Place in the preheated oven, and immediately reduce the temperature to 120°C/100°C fan/Gas ¼. Bake for 25 minutes, then turn off the oven, open the door slightly, and leave the Rolo Meringue Kisses inside to cool for at least 2 hours.

MESSY TROPICAL(ISH) TRIFLE

SERVES 4

1 quantity Cardamom Crème Pâtissière (see page 252)

For the 'cheat' madeleines
60g salted butter, melted
60g golden caster sugar
1 egg
1 tsp vanilla
50g self-raising flour
25g desiccated coconut

For the fruit layer
80ml passionfruit liqueur (or orange juice)
1 small mango
6 passionfruit
8 large strawberries
3 kiwi fruit
4 tbsp Express Passionfruit Curd (see page 251)

For the topping
400ml whipping cream
2 tbsp icing sugar
1 tbsp vanilla bean paste or extract

Essential equipment
Piping bag fitted with 10mm nozzle
12-hole madeleine tin, well greased
4 large wine glasses or cocktail glasses

It's almost impossible to get something that is literally thrown together to look remotely glamorous, so I say just make a messy one. Because I'm a baker I think over-baked madeleines make a gorgeous biscuit-cake base, but of course feel free to use shop-bought.

1 Make the crème pâtissière according to the recipe on page 252. Cover it with cling film as detailed, but don't put it in the fridge.

2 Preheat the oven to 200°C/180°C fan/Gas 6.

3 To make the 'cheat' madeleine batter, simply beat together cooled, melted butter and sugar until pale and fluffy. Throw in the egg, vanilla, flour and coconut and mix to a smooth batter. Scoop into the piping bag and pipe into the prepared madeleine tin – just spoon it in if you prefer. Bake for 10 minutes. You want these to go fairly brown. When baked, remove from the oven and tap the tin sharply on the counter so the madeleines fall out. Allow to cool completely.

4 Break up the madeleines, divide the pieces between the glasses and soak with the liqueur or orange juice.

5 Prepare the fruit: peel and stone the mango and cut into 1cm cubes. Halve the passionfruit and scoop out the pulp. Hull and cube the strawberries. Peel and slice the kiwis. Pile the fruit on top of the madeleines in the glasses, reserving a little passionfruit for the end. Spoon some curd on top, then pour over the crème pâtissière.

6 Whip the cream with the icing sugar and vanilla to soft, floppy peaks, and spoon on top of the trifles. Finish with a scattering of passionfruit pulp.

BANOFFEE CREAM HORNS MAKES 6

1 quantity of Rough Puff Pastry
  (see page 246), or 500g
  shop-bought all-butter
  puff pastry
1 egg, beaten with a pinch
  of salt, to glaze
50g golden caster sugar
Icing sugar, to dust

For the toffee sauce
150g dark muscovado sugar
100ml double cream
40g unsalted butter

For the filling
150ml double cream
2 bananas, peeled

Essential equipment
6 × cream horn moulds,
  or 6 × ice cream waffle cones
  wrapped well with foil
Baking sheet, greased and
  lined with baking paper
Disposable piping bag,
  with 1cm hole snipped
  into the end

As a child, I was always intrigued by the cream horns I saw in bakeries. I was never fond of just pastry and cream – believe it or not – but I was curious as to how they would taste. When I was allowed to try one, it was love at first bite. The flaky pastry, slightly caramelised on the outside, stuffed with floppy but fluffy cream seemed too simple to be so good. These are even better than that, and take the humble cream horn up a notch. If you do bake these with kids, it goes without saying that the caramel has to be done by an adult, and a careful one at that. And don't use not having children as an excuse not to make these; they are immensely addictive, even for adults.

Cream horn moulds are easily available online, and fairly cheap too, but if you don't have time to wait for them to arrive, wrap 6 waffle ice cream cones in foil. You'll need to be extra delicate with those, and stop the kids from nibbling at them when your back is turned.

1 Preheat the oven to 220°C/200°C fan/Gas 7.

2 Flour the worktop and a rolling pin, and roll out the pastry to 30 × 45cm. Trim the edges to neaten, then slice along the length into 6 equal strips of about 4 × 40cm. Wrap these strips around the cones: start at the point of the cone then wrap the strip of pastry around and up the cone, overlapping each twist of pastry a third over the one before it. If you have surplus at the top, snip it off; don't tuck it into the mould as you'll not get the pastry off after baking. Paint these very sparingly with the glaze, then sprinkle with a generous helping of caster sugar. Lay the pastry cones on the baking sheet, and chill for about 15 minutes.

3 Take the pastry cones from the fridge and bake for 20–25 minutes, or until a pale golden brown and

BANOFFEE CREAM HORNS CONTINUED

puffy. Remove from the oven and gently manipulate the moulds/cones out – remembering to hold the hot cones with a clean oven cloth – and allow to cool completely.

4 To make the toffee sauce, place the sugar, cream and butter in a saucepan and heat, stirring until everything melts together. Bring to the boil, again stirring, and boil for a minute, then remove from the heat and decant into a heatproof bowl to cool.

5 Place the cream in a mixing bowl and whip to soft peaks. Slice the bananas lengthways into 4, then chop into fine, small chunks and fold into the cream. Chill in the fridge for 15 minutes, then ripple two-thirds of the toffee sauce through the cream.

6 Drizzle the remaining toffee into the pastry horns, zigzagging it up the insides. Load the piping bag with the whipped banana cream, and pipe into the pastry horns, trying to make sure you get it right down to the narrow tip. Finish with a dusting of icing sugar.

GINGERBREAD SOLDIERS WITH YELLOW AND WHITE DIP
SERVES 4-8

For the gingerbread
125g unsalted butter, softened
40g dark muscovado sugar
40g light muscovado sugar
1 small egg
1 tbsp golden syrup
1 tbsp treacle
4 tsp ground ginger
2 tsp ground cinnamon
270g plain flour

For the dipping sauce
300g white chocolate,
   roughly chopped
300ml double cream
100g desiccated coconut
4 tbsp Express Lemon Curd
   (see page 251)

Essential equipment
Baking sheet lined with
   baking paper

The snack that always reminds me of being a young lad is soldiers and dippy egg. Of course, I couldn't give you a recipe for toast fingers to dip into a soft-boiled egg – so I'm giving you a gingerbread version, with a warm white chocolate and coconut dipping sauce with lemon curd. This gingerbread is a shortbread with added golden syrup, treacle and ginger.

1 Cream the butter and sugars together until the sugars have almost completely dissolved and the mixture is paler. Beat in the egg, golden syrup and treacle, then sift together the ginger, cinnamon and flour and add to mix to a stiff dough. Remove from the bowl, wrap in cling film, flatten into a disc, then refrigerate for at least 30 minutes.

2 Preheat the oven to 200°C/180°C fan/Gas 6.

3 Remove the dough from the fridge and roll into a rectangle about 23 × 28cm. Trim the edges to neaten and slice the rectangle lengthways in half. Cut each half across into 8 thin fingers and place, well spaced, on the baking sheet. Bake for 10–12 minutes, or until lightly browned at the edges. Remove from the oven and allow to cool and crisp up on the baking sheet.

4 For the dipping sauce, put the white chocolate in a heatproof bowl. Heat the cream in a medium saucepan over a high heat. When it starts to bubble at the edges, pour it over the chocolate and leave for 30 seconds, then take a whisk and mix to a smooth, glossy ganache. Stir in the coconut.

5 To serve 4 adults, divide the sauce between 4 ramekins and place a blob of lemon curd on top. For kids, do the same using 8 eggcups. Serve the gingerbread fingers alongside for dipping.

FREE-FORM PLUM TART
SERVES 8

½ quantity Rich Sweet
  Shortcrust Pastry (see page
  248) or 300g shop-bought
  sweet shortcrust
4 fresh plums, stones removed
  and cut into 5mm-thick slices
2 tbsp golden caster sugar

To glaze
3 tbsp apricot jam
20ml water

Essential equipment
Baking sheet lined with
  baking paper

This is another great recipe for making with kids. The pastry element requires precision and care, but then the little ones can test their dexterity with the sliced fruit on top, wrap up the edges, and into the oven it goes. Whilst the pastry, of course, contains butter and sugar so can't profess to be 'superhealthy', at least you know the finished product contains plenty of fruit.

1 Preheat the oven to 200°C/180°C fan/Gas 6.

2 Roll out the pastry to about 3mm thick, trim to a circle about 23cm in diameter and place on the baking sheet. Arrange the plum slices on top of the pastry, leaving a good inch bare around the edges. Sprinkle with the sugar, then fold the pastry edge up and over the fruit – this isn't a time for elegance or artistic flair, just get on with it!

3 Chill for at least 30 minutes, then bake for 30–35 minutes, or until the pastry is fairly dark, and the plum slices are yielding but not totally broken down.

4 For the glaze, boil the jam and water together, then strain to remove any lumps.

5 Remove from the oven but leave on the hot baking sheet to ensure a completely crisp pastry bottom. Paint the plums immediately with the glaze.

VANILLA AND CHOCOLATE PINWHEELS

MAKES 16–20

120g butter
60g golden caster sugar
Seeds from 1 vanilla pod
Two 90g portions plain flour
2 tsp cocoa powder

Essential equipment
Baking sheet lined with
    silicone or a double layer
    of baking paper

This is a fun recipe to make with kids. I find it comical how they struggle rolling the dough out and having it stick to the board before I step in and help them with a dusting of flour. The finished biscuits are impressive, and wouldn't be out of place on a petit four plate.

1 In a mixing bowl, or freestanding electric mixer with paddle attachment, beat the butter until it is soft. Add the sugar and vanilla seeds and beat in until pale and fluffy. Divide this mixture between two bowls, with the exact same amount in each. Into one half add 90g flour and beat until a smooth dough forms – you may need to get your hands in there to clump it together. Into the other, sift in 90g flour and the cocoa powder. Bring this together into a dough, again getting the hands in there if necessary. Flatten both doughs into separate discs, wrap in cling film, and refrigerate for at least 30 minutes.

2 When the dough is chilled, remove from the fridge and gently knead it to bring it back to a usable consistency. Roll each ball of dough out separately into rectangles about the size of A5 paper – use a light dusting of flour if necessary, but not too much. Place the chocolate sheet of dough on top of the vanilla, then trim the edges to neaten. Roll the double dough up tightly, wrap in cling film and chill for 30 minutes.

3 Preheat the oven to 200°C/180°C/Gas 6.

4 After the resting time in the fridge, cut the dough sausage into 4mm-thick discs – you should get between 16 and 20. Place these well spaced apart on the baking sheet and bake for 12–15 minutes or until the edges are just starting to turn gold. Remove from the oven and leave on the sheet to cool and crisp.

MY BAKEWELL TARTS
MAKES 6

1 quantity Shortcrust
   Pastry (see page 247)

For the jammy layer
4 tbsp jam – I use cherry
   or blackcurrant

For the frangipane
180g salted butter, softened
180g golden caster sugar
Zest of 1 lemon
3 eggs
180g ground almonds
½ tsp almond extract
   (not essence)
Flaked almonds,
   to decorate

For the icing
6 tbsp icing sugar
1 tbsp lemon juice

Essential equipment
6-hole 10cm/4-inch mini
   pie tin
Disposable piping bag fitted
   with 10mm nozzle

I questioned this recipe. I consulted my friends and followers on Twitter and asked if, as a nation, we are past the Bakewell tart. The outcry was incredible. It was as though I had declared I was going to wipe Bakewell – both town and bake – from the map of Britain. I therefore have no choice but to include the recipe. Bakewell tart, for me, is a reminder not just of my youth but of moments of solitude too. I would always enjoy a Bakewell tart, alone, with a glass of ice-cold milk. I'd take a big mouthful of Bakewell and a sip of milk, then mush it all together in my mouth.

1 Preheat the oven to 200°C/180°C fan/Gas 6.

2 Roll the pastry out and use it to line the 6 holes in the tin. Prick the bases all over with a fork, then divide the jam between them. Refrigerate until needed.

3 To make the frangipane, cream together the butter, sugar and lemon until pale and fluffy – this can be done by hand or with the help of an electric whisk or freestanding mixer. Beat in the eggs until well mixed, then add the almonds and extract and fold together. Put into the piping bag and pipe into the pastry cases, on top of the jam. Sprinkle over a few flaked almonds, before refrigerating for another 15 minutes.

4 Bake for 20–25 minutes, or until the pastry is crisp and the frangipane is baked through – a skewer inserted into it should come out clean, bar a few little almond crumbs. Remove from the oven and allow to cool completely in the tins.

5 Beat together the icing sugar and a little lemon juice at a time until you have a thick icing. Drizzle over the cooled tarts and serve.

BLACKBERRY JAM CRUMBLE SHORTBREADS
MAKES 16

For the jam
200g blackberries
200g golden caster sugar
½ tsp lemon juice

For the shortbread
300g plain flour
220g unsalted butter, softened
100g golden caster sugar

For the crumble topping
50g unsalted butter
75g plain flour
30g golden caster sugar
40g rolled oats

Essential equipment
20 × 30cm/8 × 12-inch deep-
  sided roasting tray, greased
  and lined with baking paper

When I last visited Paris, I would meander down the Boulevard Beaumarchais to an artisan baker where I would buy a slice of the most delicious sablé pastry, topped with a gooey, almost chewy jam and a delicate crumble. It reminded me of childhood, those familiar flavours of buttery shortbread and blackberry crumble coming together in one bite.

1 First make the jam. Place all the ingredients in a medium saucepan and set over a high heat. Stir until the berries begin to release their juice, and the sugar dissolves into it. Allow to boil for about 5 minutes, and make sure you stir every minute or so. You need to reach the 'thread stage'. Take the spoon out of the jam, ensuring it is slightly coated. Let it cool a little, then touch your forefinger on to the jam, and squeeze the jam gently between forefinger and thumb. When you pull your finger and thumb apart, there should be a thread of jam between them. At this stage, pour the jam into a cold bowl and allow to cool.

2 To make the shortbread, place the flour, butter and sugar in the bowl of a freestanding electric mixer fitted with paddle attachment. Mix together on a low-medium speed until the mixture comes together in a scraggy mass. Tip this into the lined tin and press it down evenly. With a fork, gently scrape down the length of the shortbread, then across the width to create a criss-cross pattern – this will help the jam cling to it. Then top with the jam and spread that out evenly too.

3 Preheat the oven to 200°C/180°C fan/Gas 6.

4 Make the crumble by rubbing the butter into the flour to create sandy breadcrumbs, then stir through the sugar and oats. Sprinkle generously on top of the jam. Bake for 35–40 minutes, or until the crumble is a gorgeous but gentle golden brown. Allow to cool before removing from the tin and slicing into 16.

WENDY'S BEETROOT CAKE
SERVES 6–8

175g fresh uncooked
  beetroot, washed
200g self-raising flour
75g sultanas
75g pecan nuts, slightly
  bashed into rough pieces
Zest of ½ large orange
1–2 tsp ground cinnamon
½ tsp fresh nutmeg,
  finely grated
1 tsp baking powder
Pinch of salt
3 eggs
175ml sunflower oil
175g soft light brown sugar

For the filling and topping
250g mascarpone cheese
150ml double cream
4 tbsp icing sugar
Ground cinnamon for dusting

Essential equipment
2 × 20cm/8-inch loose-
  bottomed cake tins, greased
  and lined with baking paper
Piping bag fitted with
  10mm nozzle

I love this cake. I judged it at a Bake Off for Avant Garden Centre in Leyland, Lancashire, near my parents' house, and it was incredible. The winner of the competition, Wendy Haydock, kindly gave me her recipe. This is not only a delicious treat for adults, it's also a brilliant cake to make with children, as not only does it demonstrate how to roast vegetables first, but it also shows how easy it is to incorporate healthy foods into something really tasty. And believe me, this is tasty.

1 Preheat the oven to 200°C/180°C fan/Gas 6.

2 Wrap the beetroot in foil and bake for 35–45 minutes, or until soft and the skin comes off easily. Allow to cool, then peel and grate coarsely.

3 Reduce the oven to 170°C/150°C fan/Gas 3.

4 Place the flour, sultanas, pecans, zest, cinnamon, nutmeg, baking powder and salt into a mixing bowl and stir together until everything is well mixed. Beat the eggs with the sunflower oil and sugar, and then add to the dry ingredients. Mix until just incorporated, then fold in the grated beetroot.

5 Divide between the prepared baking tins and bake for 40–50 minutes or until a skewer inserted into the centre comes out clean. Allow to cool completely.

6 Meanwhile, mix all the ingredients together for the filling/topping, except the cinnamon, until smooth. Once the cakes are cooled, put one on a plate. Pile the filling into the piping bag and pipe little blobs in circles to cover the top. Carefully position the second cake top-side down so the flat bottom becomes the top. Spread the remaining mixture on top, then use a fork to decorate. Dust the top with cinnamon.

PICNICS: GARDEN OR CARPET

Granted, here in the UK it's rare that we will get guaranteed weather good enough for an outdoor picnic, but why should that stop us? If it pours, then bring the picnic field into your front room and enjoy the snacky bits and pieces at home. These bakes are based on easy transportation. If that is simply carrying them from the kitchen to the lounge, so be it – at least it will be easy!

Weather wisecracks aside, there truly is no country more beautiful than Britain when the bright green fields are kissed by sunlight. Picnics, for me, are a time of nonchalance; a time to lie in the grass, nibbling all day and worrying about nothing – other than the food running out!

WALNUT, MUSHROOM, PARMESAN & ONION LOAF
SERVES 8–10

400g white bread flour
100g wholemeal bread flour
10g fast-action yeast
10g salt
220ml tepid water
100ml Guinness

For the filling
30g unsalted butter
A little oil
1 large red onion, finely sliced
Salt and pepper
1 tbsp golden caster sugar
200g chestnut mushrooms,
  finely sliced
100g walnuts, bashed
150g Parmesan cheese,
  finely grated

Essential equipment
Baking stone or baking sheet

This is a perfect picnic loaf. The bread itself not only looks attractive with its evenly spaced pleats and beautifully bronzed crust (see overleaf), but the strong, flavourful filling is perfectly protected until it's sliced – or ravenously torn apart.

1 To make the bread, simply mix together the flours, yeast and salt, then add the liquids – I usually add 2/3 of the liquid, bring it all together, then add the remaining liquid and squeeze it into a scraggy mess. Tip this out on to the worktop and knead for about 10–15 minutes, or until the dough is smooth and elastic and sufficiently kneaded according to the tests on page 15. (Or use a dough hook in a freestanding electric mixer for 8–10 minutes.) Once kneaded, place the dough into an oiled bowl and cover with a damp tea towel. Allow to rise until doubled in size; depending on the heat of the room, this could be between 1 and 2 hours.

2 Meanwhile, make the filling. Heat the butter with a little oil in a large shallow saucepan or frying pan over a medium heat. Add the onions, with a pinch of salt and pepper, and allow to cook very slowly until soft and uncoloured – about 10 minutes. Add the sugar and mushrooms and allow to cook for a further 10 minutes or so, or until the mushrooms are tender and limp. Allow to cool completely, before mixing with the walnuts and grated cheese.

3 Once the dough has doubled in size, flour the worktop lightly and roll the dough into a rectangle of about 25 × 35cm. Pile the filling on to the dough in a sausage shape down the centre. You should have a rectangle of dough with filling down the centre, and two long sides of uncovered dough. Using a sharp knife, cut the sides into equally sized thin strips. To plait the loaf, take the first strip from the left side of the dough and fold it over the filling at a 45 degree angle, pressing it into position on the other side. Repeat with the first strip on the facing side, then alternate sides until the filling is perfectly wrapped in this plaited loaf. Allow to rise for another hour.

4 Preheat the oven to 220°C/200°C fan/Gas 7, placing the baking stone or sheet inside to heat.

5 When the dough has risen for the second time, slide it on to the hot baking stone and allow to bake until golden brown and crispy on the outside – about 20–25 minutes. Allow to cool so that the filling sets inside, then slice into gorgeous, flavourful slices.

CURRIED BEEF AND SWEET POTATO PASTIES
MAKES 4

250g minced beef
120g sweet potato, peeled
  and finely diced
1 small red onion,
  very finely chopped
1 garlic clove, finely chopped
2 tsp Maldon salt
1 tsp cracked black pepper
1 tsp ground cumin
1 tsp ground coriander
1 tsp paprika
1 tsp turmeric
1 tsp ground fenugreek
½ tsp ground cinnamon
1 tsp curry powder
  (mild or spicy, as you wish)
3 tbsp olive oil
1 quantity Rough Puff Pastry
  (see page 246), or 500g
  shop-bought all-butter
  puff pastry
1 egg, beaten with a pinch
  of salt, to glaze

Essential equipment
20cm/8-inch side plate
  or cake tin, as a template
Large baking tray, lined
  with baking paper

For me, a picnic wouldn't be the same without a succulent, sizeable pasty. These not only satisfy the pasty requirement, but the mildly spiced flavour is ideal for a sunny day on the heath. These are picnicking perfection, served with a bottle of ice-cold ginger beer and a little dollop of mango chutney or sweet chilli dipping sauce.

1 Put the beef into a mixing bowl. Add the sweet potato along with the onion, garlic, salt, pepper, all the spices and the olive oil, and stir together until everything is well mixed.

2 Preheat the oven to 220°C/200°C fan/Gas 7.

3 Roll the pastry out to about 5mm thick, then cut out four 20cm discs using a tin or plate as a template. You may need to cut out two, then re-roll the pastry for the final two, but remember never to scrunch puff pastry up into a ball; layer it and then re-roll.

4 Take a quarter of the filling and squeeze it tightly into a ball. Place in the centre of one of the discs of pastry, then lightly egg wash one half of the disc. Fold the pastry over the filling, press gently to seal, then crimp: place the forefinger of your right hand on the right edge of the pasty, then with your left hand bring the pastry up and over your right finger, before pressing it down. Repeat until the entire seam of pastry is crimped.

5 Repeat with the remaining filling and pastry discs, then glaze the pasties with the beaten egg. Bake for 35 minutes, until golden brown and puffed up. These will be absolutely fine if left to cool, then chilled, and will in fact be even better the next day once the flavours have had time to develop.

CRUMBLE IN A JAR
MAKES 6

800g cooking apples
   (about 4), peeled, cored
   and cut into 1cm cubes
400g golden caster sugar
100g unsalted butter, cubed
1½ tsp ground cinnamon

For the crumble
100g plain flour
75g golden caster sugar
60g unsalted butter, cubed
50g porridge oats

Essential equipment
6 × 300ml(ish) jam jars
   with lids

Just because I'm at a picnic doesn't mean I accept food out of packets from a local petrol station. Nor does it just mean sandwiches and boiled eggs – being a greedy lad I need to know that my picnic hamper is full to bursting with sweet and savoury. These crumbles are not only incredibly simple to make, but they look great in their little glass containers, ready to be carried, opened and devoured.

1 Place half the apple cubes in a medium saucepan with the sugar and butter, and set over a high heat until the butter and sugar melt together and start to boil. Reduce to a high simmer and allow to stew until the apples just give up and turn to a gorgeous slush. At this stage, add the other half of the apples and cook until they are just tender and soft, but not slushy. Stir in the ground cinnamon. Divide the mix between the jam jars and set to one side.

2 Preheat the oven to 200°C/180°C fan/Gas 6.

3 To make the crumble topping, stir together the flour and caster sugar, then add the butter and rub into the flour until it resembles inelegant breadcrumbs. Stir through the oats, then sprinkle on top of the apple in the jars.

4 Bake the crumbles for 25 minutes, or until the apple filling is thick and bubbly, and the crumble gently golden. Allow to cool before fitting the jam jar lids and trotting off to the picnic.

RHUBARB, WHITE CHOCOLATE AND THYME TRAYBAKES SERVES AT LEAST 20

250g unsalted butter, softened
250g golden caster sugar
Leaves from 5 sprigs
  fresh thyme
5 eggs
1 tsp vanilla bean paste
  or extract
300g plain flour
1½ tsp baking powder
¼ tsp salt
200g fresh rhubarb,
  cut into 1½ cm chunks
180g white chocolate chips

Essential equipment
23cm/9-inch square baking
  tin, greased and lined with
  baking paper (or use a
  23cm/9-inch square
  disposable foil container)

I never used to appreciate the handiness of a traybake. I thought they were some form of gimmicky thing to be scoffed at rather than scoffed. But when I went on a picnic, I learnt their true value. Even more so when they are baked in a disposable foil container so that they can be portioned on the picnic site. The thyme in this may seem like an arbitrary addition, but believe me when I say that thyme isn't just for savoury foods.

1 Preheat the oven to 170°C/150°C fan/Gas 3.

2 Place the butter, sugar and thyme in a mixing bowl and beat together until the sugar has dissolved into the butter, and the mixture is pale and fluffy. You can do this in a freestanding electric mixer fitted with a paddle attachment.

3 Add the eggs one at a time, and beat well after each addition, adding the vanilla with the last egg. Sift the flour, baking powder and salt over the top and fold in, then fold in the rhubarb and white chocolate chips.

4 Pour into the prepared tin and bake for 35–40 minutes, or until golden brown and a skewer inserted into the centre comes out clean – though don't mistake a bit of soggy rhubarb or melted white chocolate for uncooked cake batter. Allow to cool and then pop into the picnic hamper – if you can wait that long.

FETA, SPINACH AND HONEYED ALMOND FILO TARTLETS
MAKES 8

2 tsp oil
1 large onion, finely chopped
Salt and pepper
200g spinach leaves
1 tsp ras-el-hanout spice blend
2 tbsp runny honey
75g flaked almonds
  (save a few for decoration)
200g feta cheese
6 sheets filo pastry,
  thawed if frozen
60ml extra virgin olive oil

Essential equipment
12-hole deep muffin tray

Eschew the run-of-the-mill foods that appear on picnic blankets countrywide in favour of these filo tartlets. They are not only slightly lower in saturated fat than a normal tartlet, but because of the sour cheese and sweet honey, along with the crunchy almonds, they are an absolutely divine addition to any picnic. Although temptation is almost impossible to resist, I urge you to allow these to cool completely before eating – that allows the honey to soak into the mixture, and for the flavours to – dare I say it – mingle.

1 Place the oil in a frying pan and set over a medium heat. Allow to warm up, then add the onion, along with a pinch of salt and pepper, and allow the onion to sweat down for a good 15 minutes, stirring occasionally, until soft and yielding. Add the spinach, ras-el-hanout and honey and stir over the heat until the spinach has wilted down. Remove from the heat and allow to cool completely.

2 Preheat the oven to 200°C/180°C fan/Gas 6.

3 When the filling has cooled, add the almonds and crumble in the feta cheese. Stir everything together until evenly combined.

4 Brush each sheet of filo pastry with the oil – using a pastry brush is easiest – then layer up on top of each other. Cut into 8 equal squares of layered pastry, then line 8 of the holes in the muffin tray with them, ensuring there is plenty overhanging at the top. Using your hands, take portions of the filling, squeeze out the excess moisture and pile into the pastry cases. Wrap the overhanging pastry over the filling to encase it. Sprinkle over a few more flakes of almonds then bake for 20–25 minutes, or until perfectly golden and crisp. Allow to cool before serving.

PICNIC PIE
SERVES 8

1 quantity Hot Water Crust
  Pastry (see page 249)

For the filling
4 large chicken breasts
8 rashers streaky bacon
2 small red onions
2 large apricots,
  stone removed
¼ tsp nutmeg
A pinch of chilli flakes
½ tsp salt
½ tsp cracked black pepper
Small handful fresh parsley,
  finely chopped
1 egg, beaten with a pinch
  of salt, to glaze

For the thick-set gelatine filling
3 gelatine leaves
300ml apple juice
A 28g chicken stock pot

Essential equipment
900g/2lb loaf tin, greased

I love a hot water crust pie. I think every book I write will contain one, and not just because I am a lad from Wigan, but also because my parents used to own a fish and chip shop – and I don't like fish and chips, so my supper of choice was always pie. I am pie mad. Any pie will do, but there is something I love about the cold, savoury slices of this one. This would be sensational served with an apple chutney, and maybe some strong Cheddar too.

1 Preheat the oven to 200°C/180°C fan/Gas 6.

2 Roll out two-thirds of the pastry and use it to line the loaf tin. Roll out the remaining third ready to be the top, and chill both loaf tin and pastry top in the fridge.

3 Finely chop the chicken breasts, bacon, red onions and apricots and mix together in a bowl with the nutmeg, chilli, salt, pepper and parsley.

4 Remove the pastry-lined loaf tin from the fridge and add the filling. Glaze the edges of the pastry lightly and add the top layer of pastry. Trim the edges to neaten and crimp to seal. Glaze the top of the pastry and make a hole about 1cm in diameter to allow steam to escape. Bake for an hour, or until a digital thermometer inserted into the centre of the pie reads about 74°C. Remove from the oven and allow to cool completely.

5 To make the thick-set jelly, place the gelatine leaves, one by one, into a jug of cold water and allow to soften for about 5 minutes. Meanwhile, heat the apple juice and add the stock. Squeeze out the excess moisture from the gelatine leaves, and add to the hot apple stock. Allow to cool slightly, then gently pour through the hole in the top of the pie, allowing each addition to sink down before adding a little more. Set in the fridge overnight.

ELDERFLOWER SOAKED LOAF WITH GOOSEBERRY & NETTLE COMPOTE

SERVES 8–10

170g golden caster sugar
100g salted butter, softened
70g full-fat Greek yoghurt,
   plus extra to serve
Zest of 1 lemon
3 eggs
170g plain flour
1 tsp baking powder

For the drizzle
2 tbsp elderflower cordial
1 tbsp lemon juice
2 tbsp granulated sugar

For the compote
200g gooseberries
200g golden caster sugar
4 large nettle leaves, left whole

Essential equipment
900g/2lb loaf tin, greased and
   lined with baking paper

Elderflower is such a refreshing flavour. It's the taste of summer for me. This loaf is almost pudding-like, thanks to the Greek yoghurt in the recipe – the acid tenderizes the crumb, which results in a soft, easy-eating loaf.

1 Preheat the oven to 170°C/150°C fan/Gas 3.

2 Place the sugar and butter in a mixing bowl and whisk until very pale and fluffy. I do this in a freestanding electric mixer with whisk attachment. Add the yoghurt and lemon zest, and whisk briefly until just incorporated, then whisk in the eggs. Gently sift over the flour and baking powder, then fold in. Scoop gently into the lined loaf tin, and bake for 40–50 minutes, or until golden brown and a skewer inserted into the centre comes out clean. Remove from the oven and allow to cool in the tin for about 5 minutes, then remove from the tin.

3 While the cake is in the tin, make the drizzle. Heat together the cordial, lemon juice and sugar until the sugar is sodden but not dissolved. When the cake has just come out of the tin, paint the top and sides with drizzle using a pastry brush. It takes a while for it all to soak in, but keep going until all the drizzle is used.

4 To make the compote, place the gooseberries, sugar and nettle leaves in a saucepan and bring to the boil, stirring so as not to burn the sugar, then reduce to a gentle simmer and cook until thick and gloopy – about 15 minutes. Remove the nettle leaves.

5 Serve the cooled cake in generous slices, topped with a little more Greek yoghurt and plenty of the compote.

COOKIE DOUGH BROWNIES
MAKES 16

For the cookie dough
40g golden caster sugar
40g light muscovado sugar
80g unsalted butter
½ tsp vanilla bean paste
    or extract
150g plain flour
1 tsp golden syrup
60g milk chocolate chips

For the brownie batter
180g dark chocolate
125g salted butter
2 eggs
3 tbsp mayonnaise
125g light muscovado sugar
85g golden caster sugar
70ml milk
Seeds from 1 vanilla pod
    or 1 tsp vanilla bean paste
    or extract
180g plain flour
3 tbsp cocoa powder

Essential equipment
Deep-sided baking tray
20cm/8-inch square cake tin
    or disposable foil container,
    greased and lined with
    baking paper

Brownies are the paradigm of picnic foods – easily sliced in their foil containers and taken to be divided amongst hungry hands on the heath. Whilst for me there is no greater love than a plain brownie, this cookie dough offering is seriously sumptuous! If, for some inexplicable reason, you have any leftovers, tear them into chunks and strew over real Italian ice cream.

1 Make the cookie dough by putting all the ingredients into a mixing bowl and beating together into a smooth, thick dough. Take walnut-sized chunks and roll into tight balls. Arrange these, well spaced, on the baking tray and put in the freezer for at least an hour.

2 Preheat the oven to 190°C/170°C fan/Gas 5.

3 When the cookie dough balls are frozen, make the brownie batter. Finely chop the chocolate, place in a heatproof mixing bowl set over a pan of simmering water and allow to melt. Dice the butter and stir into the melted chocolate until glossy. Remove from the heat and allow to cool for a minute.

4 Beat in the eggs and mayonnaise. I find it satisfying to do this with a wooden spoon, but you could transfer it all to a freestanding electric mixer if you wish. Beat in the remaining ingredients until you have a smooth, velvety batter. Put the frozen cookie dough balls into the lined square cake tin, trying to have them as evenly spaced as possible. Pour the brownie batter into the tin, over the cookie dough balls, and bake for 20–25 minutes, or until the top is cracked but the underneath still slightly soft. Allow to cool completely in the tin before slicing into chunks or wedges.

RHUBARB & ROSE SHORTS MAKES 14–16

For the jam
100g rhubarb, cut into
   5mm-thick discs
75g golden caster sugar
1–2 tbsp rosewater

For the shortbread
120g unsalted butter, softened
60g golden caster sugar
180g plain flour

Essential equipment
Baking sheet lined with a
   silicone mat, or a double
   layer of baking paper
6cm/2½-inch circle
   cookie cutter
4cm/1½-inch circle
   cookie cutter

These cookies are delicious. The rose water is an amplifier for the rhubarb. Don't worry about 'overworking' this dough; there is very little water content, and water is what is needed to form gluten in the flour. That said, though, don't go mad!

1 To make the jam, put the rhubarb and sugar into a medium saucepan with a splash of water. Set over a high heat and allow to bubble together, stirring, then reduce to a heavy simmer and allow to bubble down until thick – about 15–20 minutes. Remove from the heat and allow to cool slightly, then stir in the rosewater. Set to one side until needed.

2 To make the shortbread, beat the butter until it is smooth then add the sugar and beat that in until pale and fluffy – you can do this with a wooden spoon if you're a masochist; I prefer my handheld or stand mixer. Once the butter and sugar are well combined, throw in the flour and beat until the mixture comes together in pea-sized rubble. Squeeze the mixture into a smooth dough, and gently knead it for a moment to help it all stick together.

3 Roll out the dough to about 5mm thick. With the larger cookie cutter, cut out 14–16 discs and place on the lined baking sheet. Clump together the leftover, re-roll to the same thickness and cut out another 14–16 discs, then, this time, take the smaller cutter and cut out the centre of those discs so that you have dough rings. Place these on top of the whole dough discs – you may need to keep cutting out and clumping together the dough to get enough.

4 Preheat the oven to 200°C/180°C fan/Gas 6.

5 Spoon a scant teaspoon of the jam into the centre of each ring of dough, being as neat as possible. Bake for 12–15 minutes, or until the jam has thickened even more, and the edges of the cookies are a very pale golden. Allow to cool completely.

BAKED ARANCINI
MAKES 6

For the risotto
1 tbsp sunflower oil
1 small onion, very finely
   chopped
2 cloves garlic
1 tsp sea salt flakes
1 tsp fennel seeds
200g risotto rice (Arborio
   or carnaroli are fine)
250ml prosecco or
   dry white wine
625ml chicken stock
1 tbsp double cream
30g butter
30g freshly grated
   Parmesan cheese
Small handful fresh parsley,
   finely chopped

To assemble
1 egg
30g breadcrumbs
125g mozzarella cheese
1 small fat red chilli, deseeded
   and finely chopped
3 slices prosciutto
100g breadcrumbs mixed
   with 30g freshly grated
   Parmesan, for rolling

Greenwich Market is where I fell in love. I know, it doesn't sound terribly romantic, but the recipient of this love was neither human nor humanoid; it was merely a ball of rice. Though perhaps that underplays just how damn good these balls of rice are. I mean, think about it: risotto, clumped into spheres encasing mozzarella, chillies and prosciutto. Whilst these are verging on cookery, I've sneakily slotted them into a baking book, but believe me, when you try these you will thank me. What's more, you're really getting two recipes for the price of one here: a rich risotto, which, if not devoured, will be transformed into the adorable arancini. What I particularly love about these at a picnic is their deceit. Your picnic peers will unsuspectingly select one, thinking it a humble scotch egg, only to find a spicy, cheesy rice ball.

1 Place a large, deep-sided frying pan or sauté pan over a high heat and add the oil. Once the oil is hot and seductively shimmering, turn the heat down to medium-low and add the onions. Meanwhile, finely chop the garlic, then, using the sea salt flakes, make a paste: with the flat of the knife, gently squidge the salt into the chopped garlic until the garlic is mushy. Add to the pan and stir occasionally until the onions are soft and translucent. Add the fennel seeds and rice, mix a little to coat the grains in the oniony slick, then add half the prosecco. Allow the pan to bubble and simmer until the prosecco has almost entirely been absorbed by the rice, then add the other half. Wait again for absorption.

2 Add the stock in 125ml portions, waiting for the rice to absorb it after each addition. This takes a little

while, about 20 minutes, but just enjoy the time you can spend idly stirring the pan without a care in the world.

3 When you have used all the chicken stock, taste a spoonful. Is the rice only slightly toothsome, and clumping together? If so, you're there; if not, carry on cooking, adding a little water if you have run out of stock. Remove the pan from the heat and add the cream, butter and Parmesan, stirring until they melt into the rice. Stir in the parsley, then allow to cool completely before refrigerating.

4 To make the filling for the arancini, take the cooled risotto and put into a mixing bowl. Break in the egg and beat that evenly through the rice, along with the breadcrumbs. Chop the mozzarella into 6 even(ish) cubes, and roll each one in the finely chopped chilli. Wrap each chilli-flecked cheese cube with half a slice of prosciutto.

5 Preheat the oven to 200°C/180°C fan/Gas 6.

6 Take a small palmful of the mushy rice mix and stud a prosciutto-wrapped chunk of cheese into it. Seal that with another ball of rice mix so the cheese and prosciutto are completely encased in sticky rice. Make sure it is well compact, then place on a tray. Repeat with the remaining rice and cheese – you should get 6 arancini in total.

7 Put the 100g breadcrumbs with 30g Parmesan on to a plate and roll each arancino in them until completely coated. Place the coated rice balls on to the baking sheet and bake for 25–30 minutes, or until golden brown.

STROMBOLI BUNS
MAKES 12

500g white bread flour
10g fast-action yeast
10g salt
320ml water
30ml olive oil
Ground polenta for dusting

For the filling
6 heaped tbsp tomato purée
1 garlic clove, finely minced
½ tsp salt
½ tsp cracked black pepper
1 tsp dried chilli flakes
1 small red onion,
  very finely sliced
Small handful fresh basil,
  roughly torn
125g medium Cheddar
  cheese, coarsely grated
10 slices Prosciutto ham,
  torn

Essential equipment
12-hole deep muffin tray,
  well oiled

These spiral buns are based on the Italian classic the Stromboli, which is a loaf – similar to my Marmite and Cheddar Loaf on page 49 – that is spiralled up around a gorgeous Italianate filling. These are the ultimate bun to take on any picnic as they are crammed with flavour and easy to eat.

1 Make a simple bread dough: place the flour, yeast and salt into a mixing bowl and mix together. Add the water and mix together to a scraggy ball. Tip the contents of the bowl out and knead into a smooth elastic dough – this should take about 10 minutes. You could easily use a freestanding electric mixer with dough hook attachment, which would take about 6 minutes on medium speed. Place the dough into a well-oiled bowl, cover with a damp cloth, and allow to rise until doubled in size.

2 Whilst the dough proves, prepare the filling. Into the tomato purée mix the garlic, salt, pepper and chilli flakes.

3 Preheat the oven to 220°C/200°C fan/Gas 7.

4 When the dough has risen, sprinkle plenty of polenta on to the worktop and roll the dough out into a square of about 30 × 30cm. Spread the filling paste on to the dough, then sprinkle over the onion slices, torn basil, grated Cheddar cheese and prosciutto. Roll the dough up into a tight spiral, trim the rough ends, then slice into 12 even buns. Fit the buns into the bun tin, spirals facing up – they will be a snug fit. Allow to rest at room temperature for 30 minutes, then bake for 15 minutes.

5 Remove the buns from the oven and allow to cool and crisp in the tin, then drizzle over extra oil and pepper.

DOUBLE CHERRY & AMARETTI ROCKY ROAD
SERVES 16

200g plain chocolate
100g milk chocolate
50g butter (I use salted),
  cubed
2 tbsp golden syrup
150g dried sour cherries
200g pitted fresh cherries
150g amaretti biscuits,
  slightly crushed
75g flaked almonds

Essential equipment
20cm/8-inch square cake
  tin lined with cling film

This is one of the few things in life that gives a large reward for little effort. Melting together the ingredients, mixing and setting them, really isn't 'baking' but it tastes so darn good that to leave this out would have been a sin. This is perfect for picnics, as it can be taken in the tin it is set in – in a cool bag – and chopped into portions on site (I sometimes make it in a disposable aluminium tin for this reason). Because this recipe calls for fresh cherries, every couple of bites you'll find a refreshing burst of moist cherry, which is never a bad thing: cherries and chocolate belong together.

1 Break the chocolates into a heatproof bowl and add the butter and golden syrup. Place over a pan of barely simmering water and allow to slowly melt together.

2 Meanwhile, toss together the dried and fresh cherries, biscuits and almonds. Once the chocolate, butter and syrup have melted into a smooth, glossy liquid, pour over the cherry mixture and stir until everything is perfectly coated. Tip into the prepared tin and pat down to compact it. Wrap with cling film and refrigerate until set – at least 2 hours; overnight is preferable.

BLACK BEER & FENNEL LOAF
MAKES 1 LARGE LOAF

250g white bread flour
250g spelt flour
20g baking powder
10g salt
1 tsp fennel seeds
70g black treacle
150g natural yoghurt
250g stout (I weigh this
  because if you put it in
  a measuring jug, you have
  to wait until the froth
  subsides before you have
  a true reading)

This loaf was borne out of necessity. On one of my rare, relaxing Saturdays off, I trundled over to Borough Market in central London and bought the best brie I have ever had, along with some freshly sliced ham and a jar of chilli jam, ready for an indulgent sandwich. I got home, however, and the bread bin was bare. I made this loaf with baking powder as I simply couldn't wait for yeast to work, and all I can say is thank the Lord I was so forgetful! This is a great loaf for a picnic. Just wrap it, pack it, and when on site, slice it into thick slabs, before topping it with something succulent and delicious.

1 Preheat the oven to 220°C/200°C fan/Gas 7.

2 Place the flours, baking powder, salt and seeds into a bowl and mix together. Mix the treacle and yoghurt into the stout, then pour this into the bowl with the flour and bring together into a scraggy ball, just thicker than the thickest porridge. Tip on to the counter and form into a ball. Allow to rest for 10 minutes.

3 Place the dough on a baking sheet, and, like a soda bread, cut a deep cross into the ball. Bake for 15 minutes, then reduce the heat to 200°C/180°C fan/ Gas 6, and bake for a further 35–40 minutes, or until the loaf is deeply bronzed and sounds hollow when gently tapped on the bottom. Allow the loaf to cool before you slice, serve and smile.

LANCASHIRE BEEF HOTPOT PICNIC SLICES
MAKES 8

1 tbsp olive oil
5 stalks celery, cut
  into 5mm cubes
1 large red onion,
  very finely chopped
2 large carrots, cut
  into 5mm cubes
3 large new potatoes,
  cut into 5mm cubes
Salt and pepper
200ml hot water
400g stewing steak,
  cut into small chunks
A 28g beef stock pot
1 quantity Rough Puff Pastry
  (see page 246) or 500g
  shop-bought all-butter
  puff pastry

Essential equipment
Baking sheet lined with
  baking paper

Being a Lancashire lad, there are few things I relish more than a good, peppery hotpot. The meat is traditionally lamb, but here I'm using beef. These are very handy to take on a picnic, as the hotpot is thick and doesn't gloop around all over the hamper. Also, they are just as delicious cold as they are hot.

1 Heat the oil in a large saucepan with tight-fitting lid over a high heat and add the celery, onion, carrots and potatoes with a generous pinch of salt and pepper. Stir to coat the vegetables in the oil, then reduce the heat to low, add the water, put on the lid and sweat down for 25 minutes, stirring every once in a while. When soft, scoop the entire contents – liquid and all – into a bowl, then set the pan back over a high heat. Add the beef chunks and another small pinch of salt and pepper, and stir until browned on all sides.

2 Put the vegetables and their liquid back in the pan, stir in the stock, then reduce the heat to low. Stir well, then put the lid back on and allow the hotpot to slowly stew for 45–60 minutes until the meat is just tender – keep an eye on it and stir it occasionally, and add a little water if it seems to be drying out, but remember that you want this to be thick. Remove from the heat and allow to cool, covered, until completely cold.

3 When the hotpot is cold, preheat the oven to 200°C/180°C fan/Gas 6. Roll out the pastry on a well-floured worktop, with a well-floured rolling pin, to a rectangle of at least 32 × 36cm, then trim the edges. Cut lengthways into 4 long rectangles of 8 × 36cm, then cut each crossways in half so you have 8 rectangles of 8 × 18cm. Score inside each rectangle, just a few millimetres from the edge. Divide the hotpot amongst the rectangles, leaving those few millimetres free to rise in the oven and create a border around the filling. Bake for 25–30 minutes, or until the pastry has puffed up around the filling and is a gorgeous golden brown.

FRIENDSHIP FEASTS

What more peace can be found than just in being with friends? At the end of a treacherously tiresome week, I want nothing more than to be surrounded by my little group of buddies, laughing off the latest stresses and, most importantly, eating together. That's what we really do best. It is as though food is the glue that holds us all close. In the gang there are policemen, artists, lawyers – a very wide range of people – but when it comes to being together, food is always involved. It isn't just my obsession. Most of us love to bake, and all of us love to eat.

FIG, PECAN AND ORANGE BUNDT CAKE
SERVES 12

250g salted butter,
  at room temperature
400g light brown soft sugar
Zest of 2 medium oranges
2 eggs
300ml buttermilk
1 tbsp vanilla bean paste
  or extract
300g plain flour
2 tsp baking powder
2 tsp ground cinnamon
200g pecan pieces
200g dried figs,
  roughly chopped

Essential equipment
23cm/9-inch non-stick
  bundt tin, sprayed with
  grease spray

This is a thing of great beauty. The texture is moist like a carrot cake, but the flavour is packed with light, zesty orange, the earthy nuttiness of pecans and the gooey, malty sweetness of figs. I like to have it smeared with cream cheese and a spoonful of honey. Even better, if you manage to keep your gannet-like friends from eating every slice, this makes for perfect toast, topped with some boisterous Stilton cheese. The bundt (also known as a gugelhopf) tin you use is your choice, but I recommend one with sharply angled edges. Not only does this look impressive, but because of the sharp edges the sugars caramelize in the cake making it not crispy, but unbelievably chewy.

1 Preheat the oven to 170°C/150°C fan/Gas 3.

2 Place the softened butter in a mixing bowl and add the sugar and zest. Beat together until the sugar is well incorporated in the butter and it is fluffy.

3 Add the eggs, buttermilk and vanilla and beat in. Sift over the flour, baking powder and cinnamon, and stir in until you have a smooth batter. Fold in the pecans and figs, then scoop into the prepared bundt tin.

4 Bake for 60–75 minutes, or until a skewer inserted into the centre of the cake comes out clean. Allow to cool in the tin – this will help to create a gorgeous crust on the cake.

CURRIED BROCCOLI AND HALLOUMI FRIED NAAN BREADS

MAKES 6

For the bread
500g strong white flour,
  plus extra for dusting
10g salt
2 × 7g sachets fast-action yeast
300ml tepid water

For the curried filling
200g broccoli, trimmed
  into small florets
1 tbsp olive oil
1 medium onion, finely sliced
1 red pepper, finely sliced
1 tsp each salt and pepper
½ tsp fennel seeds
½ tsp ground fenugreek
½ tsp paprika
½ tsp mustard seeds
½ tsp ground coriander
½ tsp ground cumin
½ tsp turmeric
50ml water
1 tsp pomegranate molasses
  (or ½ tsp honey and
  ½ tsp lemon juice)
125g halloumi cheese,
  in small cubes

For frying
Sunflower oil

Essential equipment
Deep-sided frying pan with lid

Yes, you heard it right: broccoli. I love broccoli and often have cravings for it, but I know if I were to give you a recipe for broccoli flatbreads, you'd laugh my book off the shelves, so here you have it: Curried Broccoli. In all seriousness, these flatbreads really are beautiful. The pillowy, fluffy bread is a gorgeous accompaniment to the spices of the curried vegetables, then, dipped in a cooling raita dip, well, these are just manna from heaven.

1 First make the bread dough. Place the flour in a bowl and stir in the salt, then the yeast. Pour in two-thirds of the water, bring the dough into a scraggy mess, then add the remaining water and bring it together with your hands. Tip the contents of the bowl out on to the worktop and knead for 10 minutes or until smooth and elastic – or use a freestanding electric mixer fitted with a dough hook for 5–7 minutes. Place in a floured bowl, cover with a dampened cloth, and allow to rise until doubled in size – just over an hour.

2 Steam the broccoli to tender: place it into a microwavable bowl, add a tablespoon of water and cover with microwave-proof cling film. Heat on high for 3 minutes, then carefully drain the water away.

3 Heat the oil in a saucepan over a medium heat. Add the onion, red pepper, salt and pepper, and cook for about 10 minutes, stirring occasionally,

until translucent. Add the spices, mix into the pan and stir until everything is coated, then add the water and pomegranate molasses. Add the broccoli, cover the pan with the lid, reduce the heat to low and allow to cook gently for 10 minutes or so. Remove from the heat and allow to cool completely, then stir in the halloumi cubes.

4 When the dough has doubled in size, tip it out on to a lightly floured worktop and gently flatten it into a large disc. Cut into 6 equal balls. Take one ball and roll it, on a well-floured worktop using a well-floured rolling pin, into a disc of about 10cm. Take one-sixth of the filling and place it in the centre of this disc, then pull the edges of the bread over the filling to encase it and create a dough ball. Roll this out into a flatbread of about 18cm. Repeat with the remaining dough and filling.

5 When you have prepared all 6 flatbreads, heat 1 tbsp of sunflower oil in a frying pan over a high heat. When the oil shimmers, add one flatbread and fry for about 1 minute, or until the underside is nicely browned, then flip over and fry the other side for a further minute. Remove from the pan and place on kitchen paper to drain off excess oil. Quickly wipe the pan clean with a damp cloth, add another tablespoon of oil and fry the next. Repeat until you have fried all 6 naans.

MOJITO CAKE
SERVES 12–14

9 eggs, separated
450g golden caster sugar
230ml water
160ml sunflower oil
380g plain flour
1 tsp salt
3 limes, zest only

For the filling
400ml double cream
200g icing sugar
10 large mint leaves,
　finely chopped
3 tbsp white rum (optional)
1 quantity Express Lime Curd
　(see page 251)

For the topping
250g icing sugar
Juice of ½ to 1 lime
Lime zest to decorate

Essential equipment
28cm/11-inch round,
　loose-bottomed cake
　tin, ungreased
Disposable piping bag fitted
　with 10mm nozzle

This cake is absolutely perfect for long sunny evenings, and it goes without saying that it should be accompanied by a tall glass of the liquid form. The rum part is entirely optional but let's face it: without the rum there's no Mojito!

1 Preheat the oven to 170°C/150°C fan/Gas 3.

2 Place the egg yolks, sugar, water and oil in a large mixing bowl and beat together until smooth. Sift over the flour and salt and beat in along with the lime zest until well incorporated.

3 In a separate bowl, whisk the egg whites to stiff peaks, then fold gently into the batter. Pour the batter into the tin and tap the tin lightly to expel any air bubbles. Bake for 60–75 minutes, until well risen, golden and a skewer inserted into the centre comes out clean. Invert on to a wire rack to cool upside down.

4 Make the filling by whisking the cream and icing sugar to soft, floppy peaks, before folding in the mint, and rum if using.

5 When the cake has cooled, remove from the tin and slice horizontally into two even layers. Place one on a cake board or large cake stand and spread it generously with the lime curd. Fill the piping bag with the cream and pipe in neat concentric circles over the curd in two layers, then top with the other cake half – I like to use the bottom half and place it upside down so the flat bottom makes an evenly flat top.

6 Make the topping by beating together the icing sugar and lime juice, using as much juice as is necessary to achieve a spreadable but not too runny water icing – add more icing sugar or lime juice as necessary. Spread this on top of the cake and even out. Finish with a scattering of lime zest.

APPLE & GINGER HOT MERINGUES
MAKES 4

5 medium Cox apples,
 peeled, cored and chopped
 into 1cm cubes
2cm piece of fresh ginger,
 grated
125g golden caster sugar
40g unsalted butter,
 cut into 1cm cubes

For the meringue topping
2 egg whites
115g white or golden
 caster sugar

Essential equipment
4 ovenproof ramekins,
 lightly greased
Disposable piping bag fitted
 with large star nozzle

I adore an apple crumble, with its unassuming crumbly topping and sharp, molten fruit. I also adore pavlova. This dessert hits both spots. Apple and ginger is my favourite, but you could use any filling you like.

1 Preheat the oven to 140°C/120°C fan/Gas 1.

2 Place the apples and ginger in a saucepan with the caster sugar and butter, and heat over a medium-high heat. Allow the mixture to bubble gently and cook for about 20 minutes, or until the fruit juices have evaporated slightly, and the apples just yield under the pressure of a wooden spoon. Allow to cool a little, before dividing between the ramekins.

3 Make the meringue topping. Gently whisk the egg whites until they form fairly stiff peaks, then slowly add the sugar a spoonful at a time, whisking constantly. After adding the last spoonful of sugar, whisk until the meringue holds stiff peaks. Scoop the meringue into the piping bag, and pipe a high peak of meringue on to each fruit-filled ramekin. I start by piping a blob in the middle, then spiralling it out to the edges, then back into the middle, slowly piling it up into a high peak.

4 Bake for 45 minutes, or until the meringue is crispy and slightly bronzed. If you want to give it that something extra, lightly scorch the baked meringue topping with a cook's blowtorch.

SPICED HONEY LOUKOUMADES
MAKES 35–40

400g white bread flour
1 tsp salt
7g fast-action yeast
400ml warm water

For the syrup
150ml water
300g honey
1 cinnamon stick
3 bruised cardamom pods
1 star anise

A true sign of friendship for me is the ability to share, and if you can share something this good among your friends, then I hope they appreciate just how good a buddy you are. These are deep-fried Greek dough balls, poached in a spiced honey sauce. I eat them warm with Greek yoghurt, chopped pistachios, sesame seeds and a little extra runny honey.

1 Make the batter by stirring the flour, salt and yeast together in a mixing bowl, then stirring in the water using a wooden spoon. This won't be as stiff as a typical bread dough, but somewhere between bread dough and American pancake batter. Mix until smooth, then cover the bowl with cling film and leave to rise for an hour, or until the mixture has at least doubled in size.

2 Meanwhile, make the syrup by placing the water, honey, cinnamon stick, cardamom pods and star anise in a medium saucepan and heating on high. Allow to boil for at least 5 minutes, then remove from the heat and allow to infuse until needed.

3 When the batter has doubled in size, fill a saucepan about 8cm deep with sunflower oil and heat to about 180°C, using a thermometer to test the temperature. If you don't have a thermometer, you will know the oil is hot enough if, when you drop a chunk of bread into it, it floats and bubbles around the edges.

4 Drop teaspoonfuls of the batter into the oil – I do 10–12 at a time – and fry until they float to the surface and turn golden brown: 2–3 minutes. Remove the loukoumades from the oil using a slotted spoon, then drop into the syrup and allow to soak for a minute or two before removing. Serve.

LAMB LAHMAJUN MAKES 6

For the bread
400g white bread flour
7g salt
7g fast-action yeast
10g sugar
280ml tepid water

For the topping
250g minced lamb
2 cloves garlic, finely minced
1 tbsp pomegranate molasses
2 tsp sumac
2 tsp paprika
1 tsp ground cumin
1 tsp ground coriander
1 tsp sea salt flakes
1 tsp cracked black pepper
Small handful each fresh
   coriander and mint,
   finely chopped
Leaves from 4 sprigs thyme
1 tbsp sesame seeds
1 fat red chilli, deseeded
   and finely chopped

For rolling
Flour
Ground polenta or semolina

To assemble
6 tbsp hummus
90g feta cheese
Seeds of 1 small pomegranate

Essential equipment
Pizza stone (or baking sheet)
Baking sheet

These Turkish pizzas are unbelievably good, and so very moreish. This is the perfect bake for when you're having a slow, relaxed evening with friends and you all club together in the kitchen. I devour these straight from the oven, but you could easily bake them all in advance, allow them to cool, then keep them in the fridge until needed. Reheat in a 220°C/200°C fan/Gas 7 oven for 10 minutes. The list of ingredients looks long, but it's really just a case of making a basic bread dough, then topping it with the spiced minced lamb.

1 Make a basic bread dough by mixing together the flour, salt, yeast and sugar. Add the water and bring together into a scraggy ball of dough. Turn out on the counter and knead for about 10 minutes, or until smooth and elastic, or use a freestanding mixer with dough hook attachment, on medium speed for about 5 minutes. Place the dough in a well-oiled bowl, rolling it in the oil to coat it, then allow to rise until doubled in size – about 1–2 hours, depending on the heat of the kitchen.

2 Make the topping by mixing all the ingredients in a bowl – I just get my hands in there and squeeze everything together until well combined.

3 Place the pizza stone (or baking sheet) in the oven and heat to 250°C/220°C fan (gas as high as it will go).

4 When the dough has risen, remove from the bowl and divide into 6 equal portions – weighing if necessary. Dust the worktop liberally with flour and polenta or semolina, and roll out a dough portion to about 18cm diameter. Dust a baking sheet very liberally with more flour and polenta/semolina, then place the disc of dough on it – I make sure that the

LAMB LAHMAJUN CONTINUED

disc of dough moves freely and doesn't stick to the sheet before continuing.

5 Spread 1 tbsp hummus over the dough disc, leaving 1cm free around the edge. Take one-sixth of the filling and spread on top of the hummus. Crumble over one-sixth of the feta cheese, then slide the lahmajun off the baking sheet and on to the hot pizza stone/baking sheet. Bake for 12–15 minutes, or until the edges have puffed up and the base is done.

6 Repeat with the remaining dough, filling and cheese.

7 When the lahmajuns are baked, scatter with pomegranate seeds. The simplest way to get the seeds out is to slice the fruit in half, then bash each half on the back with a wooden spoon, allowing the seeds to fall through your fingers into a bowl.

FIG, STILTON, QUINCE & PROSCIUTTO PIZZA
MAKES 4 SMALL PIZZAS

For the dough
400g strong white bread flour
7g salt
15g sugar
7g fast-action yeast
280ml tepid water
30g butter, melted
Sunflower or olive oil
Extra flour and ground
   cornmeal/polenta
   for dusting

For the topping
200g Stilton cheese
100g quince jelly
12 slices prosciutto
2 large figs, sliced into eighths
Olive oil
Seeds from 1 large
   pomegranate
Fresh rocket leaves

Essential equipment
Pizza stone (or baking sheet)
Baking sheet

There really is nothing I like more than me and my group of mates teaming up to make supper. This sort of bake is perfect for that, and because the portions are individual, it is easy for the picky person – every group has one – to avoid eating something they don't like. Being a greedy guy I find it hard to believe that anyone has food they don't like, but that's just me. See overleaf.

1 For the bread dough, put the flour in a mixing bowl and stir through the salt, sugar and yeast. Add the water and melted butter and bring into a scraggy ball. Knead on the counter for 5–10 minutes, or until smooth and elastic. If you have a freestanding electric mixer, knead the dough in that using the dough hook for about 5 minutes. Roll the ball of dough around in a lightly oiled bowl, then allow to rest until doubled in size: about 60–90 minutes.

2 Place the pizza stone (or baking sheet) in the oven and heat to 250°C/220°C fan (gas as high as it will go).

3 When the dough has risen, divide into 4 equal balls. Roll one ball out into a disc of about 18cm diameter. Place this on a baking sheet that is very well dusted in flour. Crumble on a quarter of the Stilton and a quarter of the quince, drape 3 slices of prosciutto over the top, and top with 4 pieces of fig. Drizzle with a little olive oil, then slide off the baking sheet and on to the ferociously hot pizza stone, and allow to bake for 10–15 minutes, or until the edges have puffed up and are a glorious golden brown. Repeat with the remaining dough and topping. Serve with a scattering of pomegranate seeds and a few rocket leaves.

SLIMMING SUZIE'S ALMOST FAT-FREE CAKE
SERVES 10

For the genoise
4 eggs
130g golden caster sugar
Zest of 2 oranges
1 tbsp vanilla bean paste
    or extract
130g plain flour

For the soaking syrup
50ml water
50g golden caster sugar
50ml fresh orange juice

*For the Italian meringue
    topping*
4 egg whites
225g golden caster sugar
75ml water

For the fruit topping
A selection of blueberries,
    raspberries, strawberries,
    redcurrants and mint leaves
Icing sugar to dust

Essential equipment
20cm deep cake tin,
    ungreased
Sugar thermometer
Cake stand
Piping bag fitted with
    10mm plain nozzle

Every group has one: a 'slimming Suzie', one person who is 'watching their fat intake' or 'only eating 500 calories a day'. Personally, I say eat everything in moderation, but I wouldn't be so heartless as not to include a cake suitable for our Slimming Suzie. The reason this is an 'almost fat-free' cake is because there is a small amount of fat in the egg yolks.

1 Preheat the oven to 200°C/180°C fan/Gas 6.

2 To make the genoise, put the eggs, sugar, zest and vanilla into a heatproof mixing bowl and set over a pan of barely simmering water. Whisk together with a handheld electric mixer until the mixture feels slightly warm, then remove from the heat and continue whisking until the eggs have tripled in volume and you have achieved the ribbon stage – when you lift the whisks out of the mixture, the batter drips down and sits proud on the surface for at least 4 seconds. If you have a freestanding electric mixer, simply do it in that on full speed – much quicker, and no need for the warm water.

3 Sift the flour over the surface and very gently fold in, ensuring no clumps of flour lurk anywhere. Carefully pour the batter into the prepared cake tin, and bake for 20–25 minutes, or until a skewer inserted into the centre comes out clean. Remove from the oven and allow to cool in the tin until completely cold.

4 Make the soaking syrup by mixing together the water and sugar. Bring to the boil in a small saucepan

and allow to bubble for 2 minutes. Remove from the heat and allow to cool before stirring in the orange juice.

5 For the Italian meringue topping, put the egg whites in a heatproof mixing bowl – preferably metal – and whisk using a handheld electric mixer. You could also do this in a freestanding electric mixer with whisk attachment. Beat the egg whites until they are at soft peaks: when you lift the whisk out of them they *just* hold a peak, albeit a floppy one. When you reach this stage, stop mixing.

6 Place the sugar and water in a medium saucepan over a medium-high heat, and clip the sugar thermometer in place. If your thermometer doesn't have a clip, simply hold it. Do not stir the mixture at any point, just leave it to boil and bubble away. When the thermometer reads 118°C or 'softball stage' – after about 5 minutes – remove the pan from the heat immediately, being careful not to touch the sugar mixture because it's extremely hot. Turn the mixer for the egg whites back on to medium speed and continue mixing as you gently pour the sugar syrup down the side of the bowl. Continue whisking on medium until the meringue has cooled to room temperature. This will take about 6 or 7 minutes.

7 To finish, take a sharp knife and run it around the edge of the cake tin to release the cake. Slice the cake in half horizontally as evenly as possible. Place what was the top half of cake cut-side-up on a cake stand and soak it well with some of the syrup. Scoop the meringue into the piping bag and pipe a generous swirl on top. Soak the cut side of the other cake half, and place it, cut-side-down, on top of the meringue. Spoon pillowy blobs of the meringue on top of the cake, then arrange the fruit as desired. Finish with a light dusting of icing sugar.

BAKED SPICY LAMB SAMOSAS
MAKES 8

2 tbsp sunflower oil
1 large red onion,
   very finely chopped
2 medium carrots,
   very finely diced
Salt and pepper
4 fresh figs, roughly chopped
1½ tsp ground cumin
1½ tsp ground coriander
1½ tsp ground fenugreek
1½ tsp ground turmeric
1½ tsp paprika
1 tsp hot chilli powder
500g lean minced lamb
8 sheets filo pastry
1 egg, beaten with a pinch
   of salt, to glaze

Essential equipment
1 large or 2 medium
   baking sheets lined
   with baking paper

A friendship feast just wouldn't be worth having without something ultra savoury to soak up that blissful burn of booze. These samosas really are big enough to be a meal in themselves, but that doesn't stop me from adorning the friendly feast table with a batch of these beauties – beer compulsory. These can be served cold or warm.

1 Place 1 tablespoon of the sunflower oil in a large saucepan or frying pan and set over a high heat until the oil starts to shimmer. Add the onion and carrot and reduce the heat to medium-low. Add a pinch of salt and pepper, cover with a lid, and allow to cook down for 15 minutes or until the onion is very soft and the carrots are getting there too. Add the figs and cook for a further 5 minutes. Add the spices, stir over the heat for a couple of minutes, then tip the contents of the pan into a heatproof bowl and set aside.

2 Add the second tablespoon of oil to the pan and turn up the heat to medium-high. Add the lamb and cook until just brown, then add the spiced onion mix with another pinch of salt and pepper, stir for a minute, then remove from the heat and cool completely.

3 Preheat the oven to 200°C/180°C fan/Gas 6.

4 Take one sheet of filo pastry and pile one-eighth of the filling in the bottom right-hand corner. Fold the corner over the filling to start a sort of triangular shape – don't worry if it isn't perfect – then fold that up in the filo, trying to stick to a triangular parcel. Stick the excess flaps of filo down with a little water, then repeat with the remaining filo and filling, until you have 8 unbaked samosas. Glaze each one with the beaten egg, then bake for 25–30 minutes, or until the pastry is gloriously golden and crispy.

PACKED MACARONI CHEESE
SERVES 8

500g macaroni pasta
1 tsp olive oil
6 chestnut mushrooms,
   finely sliced
4 rashers unsmoked back
   bacon, chopped into
   1cm chunks
25ml vodka
4 spring onions, finely chopped
6 asparagus spears, chopped
   into 1cm chunks
½ small can sweetcorn
1 tsp salt
1 tsp pepper

For the sauce
1½ tbsp butter
1½ tbsp plain flour
650ml milk
250g Epoisses cheese, cut into
   small chunks (if unavailable,
   use a good Brie de Meaux)
70g Stilton cheese, cut into
   small chunks
100g strong Cheddar cheese,
   grated
1 tsp truffle oil

Essential equipment
Deep baking tray/dish of about
   30 × 20 cm/12 × 8 inches

This is perfect is prepared the day before and baked when required. Those of a delicate disposition should stop reading now, because I have to serve this with a ferociously hot chilli sauce – the type you'd expect to find in a kebab shop.

1 Preheat the oven to 200°C/180°C fan/Gas 6.

2 Bring a large saucepan of water to the boil, add a tablespoon of salt then plunge in the pasta and boil for 7 minutes. Drain the pasta, discarding the salty water.

3 Place a frying pan over a medium heat and add the oil. Add the chestnut mushrooms and bacon and fry, stirring occasionally, until the bacon is cooked through and the mushrooms are soft. Add the vodka, spring onions, asparagus and sweetcorn, and fry for just a minute more. Remove from the heat and toss together with the pasta, salt and pepper. Put in the baking tray.

4 To make the sauce, put the butter in a medium saucepan and set over a high heat. Once the butter has melted, beat in the flour to make a thick brown goo. On the heat, add the milk about 200ml at a time, whisking very well after each addition. Allow the sauce to come to the boil and thicken, still stirring, then reduce the heat to low and stir in the cheese, though reserve a quarter of the Cheddar for topping. Mix these in until they melt into the sauce, then stir in the truffle oil.

5 Pour the sauce over the pasta, bacon and vegetables, ensuring they are well covered. Sprinkle the remaining grated Cheddar over the top, then bake for 25–30 minutes, or until the cheese sauce is bubbling and the pasta on top is cheesy and slightly crispier.

THE ANARCHIC CHEESECAKE – PB&J
SERVES 12

I love this classic US flavour combination: peanut butter and jelly. However, whereas usually the 'jelly' component is what we'd call jam in the UK, here I've gone a step further and made a jellified jam. It needs to set, so this cake is best made the day before eating. I wrote this recipe for a magazine. Pippa Middleton was judging it and said it was 'too heavy'. With all due respect to her, if you're looking for something light, don't go near a cheesecake. (See overleaf.)

For the praline
100g golden caster sugar
2 tbsp water
150g salted peanuts

For the base
300g digestive biscuits
120g unsalted butter

For the cheesecake
750g full-fat cream cheese
150g smooth, sweet
   peanut butter
1 tsp vanilla extract
200g golden caster sugar
2 tbsp plain flour
Pinch of salt
3 eggs, separated

For the jelly top
2 gelatine leaves
340g jar seedless raspberry jam
1 tbsp water
2 tbsp cherry brandy (optional)
Salted peanuts, to scatter

Essential equipment
Foil and baking paper
23cm/9-inch deep springform
   cake tin
Roasting tray and boiling
   water, for cooking

1 First prepare the equipment. Place a large sheet of baking paper on the worktop to set the hot praline on – you may want to put this on a baking sheet to protect the work surface. Wrap the outside of the cake tin with foil to make it waterproof. Line the base of the cake tin with a circle of baking paper.

2 Preheat the oven to 180°C/160°C fan/Gas 4.

3 Make the peanut praline by placing the caster sugar and water in a saucepan. Mix together while cold, then place the pan on a high heat. Using a wet pastry brush, sweep down any sugar crystals from the sides of the pan, but don't stir the contents at any time or the mixture will crystallize. Allow to bubble away for about 5 minutes until a lovely amber colour. You can swirl the pan to ensure even browning, but don't stir. Once you have achieved the amber colour, remove from the heat, pour in the peanuts and stir until well covered. Tip this on to the baking paper and flatten down with a spoon. Allow to set until cold and brittle.

4 Make the base by blitzing the digestive biscuits to fine crumbs in a food processor, then add the butter and blitz again to a sandy rubble. Break up the peanut praline and add to the food processor, then pulse until the praline is broken up and evenly distributed among the rubble – you don't want to pulverize the praline, just break it a little and evenly disperse it.

5 Tip the contents of the food processor into the cake tin and, using a spoon, press everything down until compacted and evenly spread. Place in the fridge.

6 To make the cheesecake, place the cream cheese and peanut butter in a large mixing bowl with the vanilla. Mix together well, but gently, with a wooden spoon or spatula. Add the sugar, flour, salt and egg yolks, and beat again until smooth. Place the egg whites in a separate and clean mixing bowl, and whisk until they just hold their shape. Mix one-third of this into the cheese mixture to slacken it, then gently fold in the remaining two-thirds.

7 Take the cheesecake base from the fridge, pour the cheesecake mixture over it and place in the roasting tin. Put in the oven, but before you close the oven door, pour boiling water into the roasting dish – being careful not to splash any onto the cheesecake. Bake for 30–40 minutes. You will know the cheesecake is perfectly baked when the top has a sheen and there is a slight wobble in the middle. Remove from the oven, and from the water bath, and set on to a cooling rack until completely cool – about an hour.

8 When the cheesecake has cooled, make the jelly topping. Fill a jug with cold water and soak the gelatine leaves in it. Place the jam in a saucepan with the water and set over a medium heat. Stir as it heats to prevent the jam burning. When it is hot, but not boiling, remove from the heat and stir in the cherry brandy, if using. Take the gelatine leaves from their soaking water – they should now be very floppy – and squeeze out any excess moisture. Add to the jammy mix and stir until completely dissolved. Allow this jelly to cool for about 30 minutes before pouring over the top of the cheesecake. Cover the whole thing with cling film, though don't allow the film to touch the jelly, and place in the fridge overnight to set.

9 You can decorate the cheesecake by scattering salted peanuts over it, but I also think it is perfect with its gleaming jelly top unadorned: take your pick.

CHOCOLATE LIME PIE
SERVES 6-8

For the biscuit base
220g bourbon biscuits
50g salted butter

For the filling
397g can condensed milk
2 egg yolks
Zest of 4 limes
150ml lime juice
   (about 4 limes' worth)

Essential equipment
20cm/8-inch fluted
   loose-bottomed tart tin

Chocolate and lime is a classic combination. Just think of those citric boiled sweets, filled with a soft chocolate centre! This cake is best served cold from the refrigerator, so I recommend making it the day before. That is, if you have the self-discipline to avoid gobbling it up in the dead of night.

1 Preheat the oven to 180°C/160°C fan/Gas 4.

2 Place the bourbon biscuits and butter in a food processor and blitz to a dark sandy rubble. Tip this into the tart tin and press it down to compact it on the base and up the sides, as evenly as possible. Pop this in the fridge to chill for at least 30 minutes.

3 To make the filling, place the condensed milk, yolks, lime zest and juice in a mixing bowl and beat together. Pour that into the chilled biscuit base and then bake for 20–25 minutes, or until when nudged it trembles only slightly, but is substantially more solid than before it went in the oven.

4 Remove from the oven and allow to cool completely, before refrigerating for at least 2 hours before serving.

CHERRY PECAN PIES MAKES 6

1 quantity Rich Sweet
   Shortcrust (see page 248)
   or 500g shop-bought
   sweet shortcrust
120g unsalted butter
200g dark muscovado sugar
30g black treacle
50g golden syrup
2 eggs
3 tbsp cherry brandy
300g pecans
60g dried sour cherries

Essential equipment
6-hole 10cm/4-inch
   mini pie tin

I love pecans. Better still, there is an element of guilty, pleasurable corruption here: soaking the nuts in gooey, sugary butter, then baking them so they become a little softer, encased in a crispy pastry. This recipe is for my mate Ben, who absolutely adores pecan pie, though I haven't baked it for him yet. Sorry, Ben!

1 Preheat the oven to 200°C/180°C fan/Gas 6.

2 Roll out the pastry and cut out discs big enough to line the pie tins with (find a small saucer or tub and use as a guide). Use the discs to line the pie dishes, then prick the bases with a fork. Place into the fridge to chill.

3 To make the filling, put the butter, sugar, treacle and golden syrup into a medium saucepan and set over a medium heat. Stir constantly until the butter melts and the sugar dissolves into the mixture. Remove from the heat and allow to cool slightly, before beating in the eggs and brandy.

4 Remove the lined pie tin from the fridge and arrange the pecans and cherries so that they come to the top of each hole. Pour over the melted mixture, allowing it to soak down to the bottom before topping up.

5 Bake for 25–30 minutes, or until the filling has set. Allow to cool in the tins to help crisp up the base.

SPECIAL OCCASIONS

While I love an easy Friday night, unplanned and unfolding, I absolutely adore the bigger events of the year: the ones we can plan for and look forward to. I love Christmas so much, for example, that in June I sometimes feel prematurely festive enough – or perhaps it's Yule-starvation I'm appeasing – to watch my entire collection of Christmas cookery shows. Weddings are another joy. I like to get my sleeves rolled up and bake for those. My Wedding Hearty Rings and my modernist Splash Celebration Cake make for impressive yet achievable masterpieces. Whatever the occasion – birthday, Christmas, wedding or Valentine's – in my life there is always a bake to behold.

CHRISTMAS SPICED SAVARIN SERVES 10–12

225g plain flour
½ tsp salt
40g golden caster sugar
7g fast-action yeast
4 eggs
30ml milk
120g unsalted butter,
   at room temperature
Zest of 1 large orange
Zest of 1 large lemon
1½ tsp mixed spice
75g flaked almonds

For the syrup
220g golden caster sugar
150g cranberry juice
1 cinnamon stick
1 slice of the orange
   used for zest
1 tbsp cherry brandy

To decorate
The orange used for zest,
   segmented
The seeds of 1 pomegranate
Scattering of flaked almonds
   and pistachios
Icing sugar, to dust

Essential equipment
20cm/8-inch savarin mould,
   with butter for greasing

If you're not a fan of a Christmas fruitcake – and it seems that many people aren't, these days – then this is a fabulously festive alternative. Savarin is a sort of cake–bread hybrid. It's a cake batter, leavened with yeast. What's more, although it's kneaded like a bread to form a strong gluten network, its texture is akin to cake. The ring in which a savarin is baked is for both visual appeal and to support its structure.

1 To make the savarin batter, place the flour in a mixing bowl and stir through the salt, sugar and yeast. Put the eggs and milk in a jug and beat together. Pour this into the dry ingredients and, using a wooden spoon or handheld mixer, beat for about 5 minutes. You could do this in a freestanding electric mixer with paddle attachment. After about 5 minutes, add the butter in cubes, and beat well to incorporate into the mixture until it is smooth, elastic and satiny.

2 When the butter is well incorporated, add the orange and lemon zests, mixed spice and almond flakes, and mix in until evenly distributed. Cover the bowl with a cloth and leave the batter to prove for 1 hour.

3 Meanwhile, grease the savarin mould with butter and place it in the freezer for 10 minutes. Then grease it again and freeze until needed. This double greasing helps to ensure the baked savarin does not stick to the tin.

4 When the batter has rested for 1 hour, remove the savarin mould from the freezer and dust with a generous amount of caster sugar all over the inside.

CHRISTMAS SPICED SAVARIN CONTINUED

Spoon the batter into the mould and even it out. Cover with oiled cling film and leave to rise for another hour.

5 Preheat the oven to 200°C/180°C fan/Gas 6.

6 When the batter has risen, bake for 20–25 minutes, or until the savarin has risen up out of the tin and is golden brown.

7 Meanwhile, make the syrup by heating the sugar and cranberry juice in a medium saucepan over a high heat. Bring to the boil, then turn the heat down to low. Add the cinnamon stick, orange slice and cherry brandy and allow to infuse for 5 minutes or so. Remove from the heat and place to one side for later.

8 Remove the savarin from the mould and pour about a third of the syrup into the mould (remove the cinnamon stick and orange slice from the syrup first). Gently return the savarin to the mould so that it can start to soak up the spiced syrup. Pour the remaining syrup into a deep-sided baking tray, then place the savarin upside down in the syrup, and leave to soak for about 5 minutes.

9 Remove the mould, place the savarin on a serving plate, and decorate with orange slices, pomegranate seeds, flaked almonds, pistachios, and a snowy sifting of icing sugar.

ROSE AND RASPBERRY CREME BRULEE
SERVES 2

10 raspberries, thawed
   if frozen

For the custard
250ml whole milk
50g golden caster sugar
½ tsp rosewater (or a little
   more to taste)
Pink food colouring (optional)
3 egg yolks
2 tbsp Demerara sugar,
   to finish

Essential equipment
2 ovenproof ramekins
Roasting tray and boiling
   water, for cooking
Cook's blowtorch

I think crème brûlée is so romantic. Breaking through the caramelized sugar crust and plunging into the set custard is nothing short of lovely, and if you served this to your Valentine, I can guarantee that they will still be around a year later. My rose and raspberry version is so delicious it would stop even Cupid in his tracks.

1 Preheat the oven to 170°C/150°C fan/Gas 3 and divide the raspberries between the 2 ramekins.

2 Put the milk and half the caster sugar in a medium saucepan and heat gently until you can't quite hold your finger in it. Remove from the heat and add the rosewater, tasting to ensure it is perfectly perfumed. Add a drop of food colouring, if using, and mix to a pale pastel pink. Set aside until needed.

3 Place the egg yolks and remaining caster sugar in a mixing bowl and whisk together until the eggs turn a little paler and the sugar has dissolved. When the eggs are pale and fluffy, slowly pour in the milk mixture while continuing to whisk gently. Divide this between the ramekins and place in a roasting tray or dish. Fill the dish with enough hot water to come halfway up the side of the ramekins, then bake for 40–45 minutes, or until the custard is just set with a very slight wobble in the middle. Allow to cool completely before refrigerating for at least 2 hours.

4 Just before serving, remove the custards from the fridge and sprinkle each with Demerara sugar, shaking the ramekins so that the sugar is evenly distributed. Using a cook's blowtorch, caramelize the sugar until it melts and chars slightly. If you don't have a blowtorch, place the custards under a hot grill until the sugar has melted and darkened, being careful not to burn it too much as this will make it bitter. Serve immediately.

PISTACHIO AND WHITE CHOCOLATE CHRISTMAS TREE TORTE

SERVES 8

125g salted butter
125g icing sugar
100g Pistachio Paste
  (see page 249)
2 eggs
125g plain flour

For the ganache
350g white chocolate,
  roughly chopped
150ml double cream

Essential equipment
33 × 23cm/13 × 9-inch
  Swiss roll tin, greased and
  lined with baking paper
Baking sheet
Square cake board to
  help assembly
Long serrated knife –
  preferably a confectioner's
  knife

I'm all for the kitsch red-and-whites of traditional Christmas, but as a 'patisserie graduate' I can't help but fiddle with ideas and make alternative offerings. This torte is ultra modern, and its sweet flavour and firm texture make it very good with a mug of hot chocolate. You might glance down this recipe and think that I'm mistaken with the flour – where is the raising agent, you ask. The reason I'm using plain flour here is because the torte is layered and then cut on a diagonal. If aerated with baking powder, the structure would be too weak to hold the shape. This torte isn't dry, though. It is dense and indulgent.

1 Preheat the oven to 200°C/180°C fan/Gas 6.

2 Beat the butter until pale and fluffy either with a handheld electric whisk, or freestanding electric mixer fitted with paddle attachment. Add the icing sugar and stir through to avoid causing a giant cloud of sweet sugar smoke, then beat again until well incorporated and smooth. Stir in the pistachio paste until well mixed, then beat in the eggs. Finally, fold through the flour.

3 Scoop into the Swiss roll tin, level off, and bake for 12–15 minutes, or until a gentle golden brown. Remove from the oven and allow to cool completely.

4 Meanwhile, make the ganache: place the chocolate in a heatproof bowl. Put the cream into a small saucepan and set over a high heat. When the cream

PISTACHIO AND WHITE CHOCOLATE CHRISTMAS TREE TORTE CONTINUED

starts to bubble around the edges, pour it over the chocolate and leave to melt for 30 seconds. Using a whisk, beat it to a smooth glossy ganache. Tip the ganache out on to a baking sheet and spread it out. Allow to cool until it is the consistency of chocolate spread.

5 Take the torte from the tin and trim a few millimetres from each edge. With the cake placed horizontally before you, slice into 4 equal rectangles, side by side.

6 Spread 3 tablespoons of ganache over one of the rectangles of torte. Place another rectangle evenly on top, then put into the freezer for 5 minutes – I use the cake board here to help stabilize it all. After this time, repeat with more ganache and the next piece of torte, then chill for 5 minutes, then spread another 3 tablespoons of ganache over, and top with the fourth and final piece of torte. Place into the freezer again for 20 minutes to firm up. Don't chill the remaining ganache; it would stiffen too much.

7 When the torte is chilled and firm, take it out of the freezer and place it on the worktop: the layers will be horizontal. With great care, slice the torte in half on a diagonal into two triangular pieces. Align the pieces so that the backs are touching and the stripes of torte are vertical. Spread ganache on the back of one of the triangles, then stick them together. Chill again for another 5 minutes, then remove and spread the ganache over the sloping sides. Get it as smooth as possible – heat a small palette knife in a jug of hot water and use that – then chill again in the fridge.

8 When ready to serve, trim off the exposed ends, then slice the torte into 8 slices.

PUMPKIN AND FETA PIE
SERVES 6–8

About 1kg pumpkin flesh,
  peeled and deseeded,
  cut into 2cm cubes
6 sprigs fresh thyme
4 garlic cloves, unpeeled
  but remove the wafery skin
1 large onion, peeled and
  cut into 8 wedges
250ml stock, chicken or
  vegetable is best
1 tsp sea salt flakes
1 tsp cracked black pepper
1 tsp golden caster sugar
1 tsp cider vinegar
200g feta cheese, cut
  into 1cm cubes
1 medium-sized aubergine,
  cut into 2cm cubes
1 quantity Rough Puff Pastry
  (see page 246) or 500g shop-
  bought all-butter puff pastry
1 egg, beaten with a pinch
  of salt, to glaze

Essential equipment
30 × 20cm/12 × 8-inch
  deep-sided roasting tray
  or enamel pie dish

For Halloween, of course, I wanted to include a recipe for pumpkin pie, but I'm going to let you in on a little spooky secret: I don't like pumpkin pie. Not the regular, claggy, nutmeg-riddled kind, at any rate. I love pumpkin, just not when it's turned to a mush. This recipe embodies the gorgeous sweetness of pumpkin in savoury form, which, in my humble opinion, is the best way. Feta and thyme are the ultimate accompaniments to sweet, orange nuggets of pumpkin.

1 Preheat the oven to 220°C/200°C fan/Gas 7.

2 Place the chopped pumpkin, thyme, garlic, onion, stock, salt, pepper, sugar and vinegar into the roasting dish, wrap tightly with foil and bake for 1 hour, or until the pumpkin flesh is very soft. Remove from the oven and allow to cool completely. Remove the sprigs of thyme. Squeeze the soft garlic out of its skin and into the filling.

3 Once the filling is cool, add the feta cheese and aubergine.

4 Roll out the pastry on a floured worktop until big enough to cover the roasting dish, then put it into place, pressing the edges around the dish to seal it. Make three holes in the top, glaze well with the beaten egg, then return to the oven for about 40 minutes, or until the pastry is golden brown and puffy.

SUMMER CELEBRATION TART SERVES 12–16

1 quantity Rich Sweet
 Shortcrust Pastry
 (see page 248)

For the filling
300g white chocolate,
 roughly chopped
100ml single cream
250g mascarpone cheese
Zest of 1 lemon
5 large fresh mint leaves,
 very finely chopped

For the topping
600g raspberries, as fresh
 and firm as possible
5 tbsp raspberry jam, seedless
1 tbsp sweet white wine
 (or water)
Small handful of tiny
 fresh mint leaves
Icing sugar, to dust

Essential equipment
30 × 20cm/12 × 8-inch
 Swiss roll tin
Disposable piping bag fitted
 with number 2 nozzle

Whenever we get a rare hot and sunny day here in the UK, I for one am outside on the lawn in my shorts, if not in the kitchen mixing up something with which to hail the sunshine. This tart is a celebration of summer.

1 Preheat the oven to 200°C/180°C fan/Gas 6.

2 Roll out the pastry and use to line the Swiss roll tin, pressing well into the corners and folding the excess over the edges. Prick the base with a fork and place in the fridge for at least 20 minutes, or the freezer for 10. Line the pastry with baking paper or foil, and fill with baking beans or rice. Bake for 20 minutes. Remove the baking beans and lining, and return to the oven for a further 10–15 minutes or until golden brown and dry. If the base puffs up, press it down while hot and return to the oven. Remove from the oven and use a serrated knife to saw off the excess pastry. Allow to cool completely while you make the filling.

3 Put the chocolate in a heatproof bowl. Heat the cream in a small saucepan over a high heat until it just begins to bubble around the edges, then pour it over the chocolate and leave to melt, undisturbed, for about 1 minute. Whisk to a smooth ganache and allow to cool for 20 minutes. When cool, stir in the mascarpone cream, along with the lemon zest and mint leaves. Scrape into the baked, cooled tart shell and smooth over. Line up the raspberries in neat rows, positioning them upside down like little cups.

4 Beat the jam with the wine (or water) and put this into the piping bag. Gently fill each raspberry hole with a blob of the jam, being very diligent to ensure it doesn't dribble over the tops. Finish with a scattering of tiny mint leaves, and a dusting of icing sugar.

SPLASH 3-TIER CELEBRATION CAKE
SERVES 60–70

For the 30cm cake board
250g fondant icing
1 tbsp apricot jam
Cornflour, to dust

For the icing blobs
1 egg white
250g icing sugar
Lemon juice

For the splashes
1 egg white
250g icing sugar
Lemon juice
Red, blue, green and
  yellow food colouring

Equipment for assembly
  and decoration
3 round deep cake tins,
  one 25cm/10-inch,
  one 20cm/8-inch,
  one 15cm/6-inch,
  all greased and lined
6 round thin cake boards,
  two 15cm/6-inch,
  two 20cm/8-inch,
  one 25cm/10-inch,
  one 30cm/12-inch
String, for measuring
2 smoothing paddles
10 cake dowling rods or
  plastic drinking straws
Disposable piping bag
  with number 2 nozzle
4 paper cups or ramekins
4 forks

The beauty of this cake, whether it's used for a birthday, wedding or other celebration, is that the messier the colour splashes, the better it will look. The flavours of the three cakes, from top to bottom, are: white chocolate and raspberry, chocolate and orange, and lemon. I took inspiration for this from Chris Murphy, at Tuck-Box Cakes, who is a true artist.

1 Preheat the oven according to the table opposite.

2 To make the cakes, follow the table opposite, simply creaming the butter and sugar together for each cake until paler in colour and fluffy in texture. Add the zest if the recipe calls for it, along with any cooled, melted chocolate as required. Beat those in until well incorporated, then beat in the eggs. Finally, sift over the flour (and cocoa powder if called for) and fold those in until you have a smooth batter. Pour into the prepared tin and bake at the stated temperature for the stated time, or until a skewer inserted into the centre comes out clean. Allow to cool for 15 minutes in the tin, then remove and cool completely.

3 For the cakes that require a drizzle, make that by dissolving the sugar in the juice.

4 To make the buttercream, whisk the butter until pale and fluffy, then beat in the icing sugar until incorporated. Finally, whisk for a good 5 minutes, until very pale in colour – almost white – and aerated. In the last 30 seconds of whisking, add the zest, then at the very end add the juice – you don't want this to split the fats. Set to one side until needed.

5 To make the ganaches, roughly chop the chocolates and place in separate, heatproof bowls. Put the cream into a saucepan and set over a high heat until it starts

	25CM LEMON CAKE	20CM CHOCOLATE ORANGE CAKE	15CM WHITE CHOCOLATE AND RASPBERRY CAKE
Salted butter	450g	225g	170g
Golden caster sugar	450g	225g	170g
Zest	3 lemons	1 large orange	
Chocolate		100g dark, melted and cooled	75g white, melted and cooled
Eggs	8	4	3
Self-raising flour	450g	200g	170g
Cocoa powder		25g	
Oven preheat temp.	170°C/150°C fan/Gas 3	180°C/160°C fan/Gas 4	180°C/160°C fan/Gas 4
Drizzle/jam	Juice of 3 lemons 100g golden caster	Juice of 1 orange 50g golden caster	75g raspberry jam
Filling	BUTTERCREAM 350g unsalted butter 700g icing sugar Zest of 3 lemons Juice of 1 lemon	GANACHE 300g dark chocolate 200ml double cream Zest of 1 orange	GANACHE 300g white chocolate 125ml double cream
Time	45–60 minutes	25–35 minutes	20–30 minutes
Ready-to-roll Fondant icing	1kg	750g	500g

to bubble just around the edges. Pour the hot cream over the chocolate and let it melt for 30 seconds, then stir with a whisk until you have a smooth, glossy ganache – add the zest for the orange cake now to the dark chocolate and whisk in. Pour on to baking trays or plates and allow to cool until each is the consistency of chocolate spread (see ganache tips on page 12).

6 To assemble the cakes, trim any domed tops off, and then cut each one horizontally in half as evenly as possible. For the cakes that require drizzle, paint a liberal amount over each half. Place one half of the cake on to the corresponding cake card – gluing it in place with a little buttercream or ganache. Spread

SPLASH 3-TIER CELEBRATION CAKE CONTINUED

some of the required filling – buttercream or ganache – over the cake, then top with the remaining half – for the raspberry cake, spread the raspberry jam on to the bottom cake first. Use the remaining filling to cover the top and sides of the cake, getting it as neat and sharp as possible – see page 12 for a more detailed description on how to mask a cake.

7 To cover the cakes with the fondant icing, cut a piece of string for each cake that is the length of the diameter and two sides of the cake. Knead the fondant icing with clean hands to soften it. Dust the work surface with a liberal covering of cornflour, then roll the icing out into a circle that is just a little larger in diameter than the piece of the string for the cake. Brush the fondant with the pastry brush to remove excess cornflour, then roll it around the rolling pin, brushing the underside as you roll it. Unroll the fondant on to the cake, ensuring you don't get too much, or too little, on the starting edge. With your hands gently flatten the top surface of the fondant, then smooth the fondant down the sides – it is possible to get the fondant to adhere smoothly to the side without any pleats, though if you find it difficult, gently snip a little fondant out at the side, then bring the join together to conceal. Trim the surplus off from around the edge. Using the paddles, smooth the top and sides of the fondant out as neatly as possible.

8 To cover the 30cm cake board, paint it with apricot jam, then roll out the extra 250g of the fondant icing as above. Place the fondant on to the cake board and smooth out, then trim the surplus.

9 To assemble the cake, place the 25cm cake on to the lined 30cm cake board. Take the second 20cm cake card and place that in the very centre of the 25cm cake. With a knife, make 4 faint indentations in the icing using the circumference of the cake board as a guide. Remove the cake board, and insert 5 dowels into the bottom cake, within the perimeters of the

SPLASH 3-TIER CELEBRATION CAKE
CONTINUED

4 marks. Snip the dowels so that they fit perfectly into the cake – they mustn't pop out over the icing, then gently place the 20cm cake on to the bottom cake. Repeat this process with the middle and top cakes.

10 To pipe the icing blobs around the bottom edges of the cakes to conceal the gaps, beat the egg white slightly to break it down, then sift over the icing sugar and beat in, using a little lemon juice to slacken if necessary – you need it to be thick but pipe-able. Put into the piping bag fitted with the nozzle, and pipe even-sized blobs around the edge of each cake.

11 Now for the fun part – make another batch of icing following the instructions in step 10 – though make it just a touch thinner than the piped icing, but not runny. Then divide into 4 cups or ramekins and colour each with the colourings to a rich, bold colour. Dip forks into the icing, then splash them, with a flick of the wrist, at the cake to cover in colourful splashes. Perhaps cover the kitchen walls with newspaper first!

MY CHRISTMAS CAKE
SERVES 14

250g dried prunes, chopped
250g dried apricots, chopped
250g black raisins
150g glacé cherries, halved
250ml whisky
250g salted butter, softened
200g light muscovado sugar
50g golden syrup
30g black treacle
4 eggs
250g plain flour, sifted
  with 2 tsp mixed spice
100g ground almonds
200g pecan halves,
  roughly chopped
Zest 1 large orange
Zest 1 lemon
Brandy, to sprinkle

Essential equipment
24cm/10-inch springform
  cake tin, greased and lined
  with baking parchment,
  with an excess of about 5cm
  poking out. You must then
  grease the parchment using
  a pastry brush and some
  flavourless oil.
Skewer

Love it or loathe it, Christmas cake is a necessity during the festive period. Whether you eat it or simply use it as a Yuletide adornment, to omit this from your jubilations would be sinful; and I would go right off you were you to do so. This is not a dark fruit cake as you'd expect a Christmas cake to be; it is a little lighter. Fanny Cradock would have referred to it as a 'White Christmas Cake'. I make it well in advance (towards the end of October) and feed it once a week with brandy. It must be wrapped exceedingly well in cling film and plenty of foil.

1 Put the prunes, apricots, raisins and cherries in the whisky, cover and soak for at least 5 hours.

2 Preheat the oven to 160°C/140°C fan/Gas 3.

3 In a large mixing bowl, cream the butter and sugar until light and fluffy. Mix in the molasses and treacle. Add one egg and then one-quarter of the sifted, spiced flour and ground almonds, mixing well after each addition. Continue this process until all the flour, almonds and eggs are used.

4 Mix the pecans, both zests and the soaked fruits and their soaking liquor into the batter. Pour into the prepared tin and cover with a disc of baking paper with a small hole cut into it to let out steam. Bake for about 4 ½ hours, but do check it after 3 hours or so as cooking time depends on how hot your oven burns. It will be ready when a skewer inserted into the centre comes out clean, or when the cake stops 'hissing'.

5 When the cake is completely cooled, stab it about 10 times with a long skewer, drizzle 2 tablespoons of brandy all over it, then wrap in 2 layers of baking paper and 2 layers of kitchen foil, and store in an airtight tin. Every week sprinkle 2 tbsp brandy over the cake, rewrap, and store in the same way.

MARZIPAN BRIOCHE CROWN
SERVES 16–18

250g white bread flour
Zest of 1 large orange
Zest of 1 lemon
5g salt
7g (1 sachet) fast-action yeast
30g golden caster sugar
150g egg (about 3)
20ml milk
The seeds from one
    vanilla pod
125g unsalted butter,
    softened
180g marzipan
1 egg, beaten with a tiny
    pinch of salt, to glaze

For the topping
125g icing sugar
2 tsp orange juice

Essential equipment
20cm/8-inch savarin
    mould, greased

Brioche and marzipan have to be the ultimate in Christmas flavour combinations for me. The buttery, fluffy brioche is so light, and it goes so well with a sweet nutty chunk of marzipan.

1 Make the brioche dough. Place the flour, zests and salt into the bowl of a freestanding electric mixer (one with a dough hook) and stir together. Add the yeast and sugar and blend them through too. Beat the eggs with the milk and vanilla, and add to the bowl. Gently mix together before turning the mixer on so that the flour doesn't explode everywhere when the mixer starts. Knead on a medium speed for 15 minutes, until the dough is extremely stretchy.

2 Slowly add the butter piece by piece, mixing still on medium. It should take around 5 minutes to incorporate the butter and, when done, allow the mixer to continue for about 5 minutes until the dough is smooth, silky and very stretchy indeed.

3 Place the dough on a greased baking tray and wrap tightly with cling film. Place into the fridge overnight, or for at least 12 hours.

4 Remove the dough from the fridge and divide into 9 balls of 55g. Divide the marzipan into 9 balls of 20g. Press the dough balls down into flat discs, working quickly so they don't become too sticky, and place a ball of marzipan in the centre of each. Bring the edges of the dough over the balls of marzipan to create little parcels, and arrange in the mould, seal-side down. Allow to rise until the tops of the balls just reach the top edge of the mould – this can easily take 3 hours.

5 Preheat the oven to 200°C/180°C fan/Gas 6.

6 Glaze the crown lightly with the egg wash, and bake for 25–30 minutes, or until deeply bronzed. Allow to cool completely before removing from the tin. Then beat the icing sugar and orange juice until smooth, and dribble on top of the crown, allowing it to run down the sides.

MINI GINGERBREAD TEACUP HOUSES MAKES 6

For the gingerbread
125g unsalted butter, softened
40g golden caster sugar
40g dark muscovado sugar
1 tbsp treacle
1½ tbsp golden syrup
1 small egg
220g plain flour
1 tbsp ground ginger
1 tsp ground cinnamon

For the royal icing
1 egg white (or 30g pasteurized
   egg white from a bottle if
   for children or the elderly)
About 250g icing sugar
Lemon juice, to slacken

To decorate
Hundreds and thousands
Assortment of jelly sweets
Mini chocolate drops

Essential equipment
Baking sheet lined with
   baking paper
Disposable piping bag fitted
   with small star or number
   2 piping nozzle
The template on page 192

When Christmas comes and the cups of tea and hot chocolate are plenty, these mini gingerbread houses, slotted on to the side of that warm teacup, add even more feelings of Christmassy cheer. Assembling these little houses is a fiddly task, so the more people taking part, the merrier.

1 Preheat the oven to 200°C/180°C fan/Gas 6.

2 Beat the butter and sugars together until well combined and fluffy. Add the treacle, syrup and egg and beat together. Sift over the flour, ginger and cinnamon and mix to a fairly stiff dough. Wrap in cling film, flatten into a disc and chill for 30 minutes.

3 With a well-floured worktop and a rolling pin, roll out the dough so it is about 4mm thick. Cut out 12 of each shape in the template overleaf: 12 roof tiles; 12 gables; 12 fronts – remember to cut out the shaded slots in the fronts too, as they are what will hook on to the mugs. Arrange these on a baking sheet and bake for 7–9 minutes, or until just browning around the edges. Remove from the oven but leave on the hot baking sheet to cool and crisp.

4 To make the royal icing, lightly whisk the egg white to break it down, then sift over the icing sugar and beat to a smooth, thick glue with a wooden spoon. If it's a little too thick, add a drop of lemon juice at a time. To keep it from drying out, place a damp piece of kitchen paper on the surface of the icing.

5 To assemble, put the icing into the piping bag. Pipe a line of icing on to one of the edges (on the very thin

MINI GINGERBREAD TEACUP HOUSES CONTINUED

edge itself) of a 'front' piece of gingerbread. Stick this at right angles to one of the gable pieces and hold it there for a few minutes until it adheres. Then take another 'front' piece, pipe icing on one edge, then hold that too at right angles to the other gable piece. Pipe icing on to the remaining exposed edge of the front pieces, then hold another gable piece against these so that it sticks – you should have a little house without a roof at this stage. When the icing has dried, pipe icing on to all of the thin edges exposed – so the triangle side of the gable pieces and the top edges of the front pieces. Gently place the roofs on and hold them for a few seconds until they adhere.

6 To finish, pipe icing on to the roofs and sprinkle over some hundred and thousands, and stick some jelly sweets on to the front to look like windows. Use jelly sweets and little chocolate drops to make chimneys.

7 To serve, simply slot the houses on to the rim of a teacup.

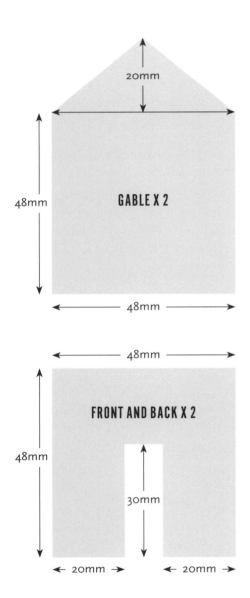

GABLE X 2

20mm
48mm
48mm

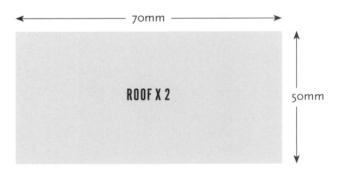

FRONT AND BACK X 2

48mm
48mm
30mm
20mm
20mm

ROOF X 2

70mm
50mm

WEDDING HEARTY RINGS
MAKES ABOUT 25

For the biscuit
65g salted butter, softened
125g golden caster sugar
200g plain flour

For the icing
1 egg white
250g icing sugar
Lemon juice, to slacken
Food colouring if desired –
 though I like a 'white'
 wedding

Essential equipment
7.5cm/3-inch heart cookie
 cutter (I measure from
 top to bottom)
5cm/2-inch heart cookie cutter
Disposable piping bag fitted
 with number 2 nozzle

I'm sure we all remember sweet, crisp, party ring biscuits. I for one used to devour them secretively as a child. I loved them, and so did many others I know. These more 'sophisticated' Hearty Rings make for a perfect choice for wedding favours – two per person coupled up in a bag, tied with a bow. What's more, this recipe is such a simple one that it is very easily multiplied or divided – so whether you've got an abundance of wedding guests or just a handful of family, you can treat them to a lovely, and inexpensive, nibble. (See overleaf.)

1 Preheat the oven to 200°C/180°C fan/Gas 6.

2 Put the butter into a mixing bowl and beat until very smooth. Add the sugar and beat until the sugar is dissolved and the mixture is fairly pale in colour. Toss in the flour and beat until the mixture starts to lump together, then tip out on to the counter and knead to a coherent dough – there's little chance of this dough being overworked because there is only butter used in it. Flatten the dough down into a disc and roll out to about 5mm thick – if it's too soft to roll, wrap in cling film and chill for 15 minutes or so then try again.

3 With the dough rolled out, cut out as many of the larger hearts as possible, then cut out the centre of those hearts using the smaller cutter. Clump the leftovers together and re-roll. Arrange evenly on a baking sheet – I recommend doing the rolling and cutting on a baking sheet so that you don't have to move the delicate little hearts about – and bake for 8–10 minutes, or until gently golden. Remove and allow to cool and crisp on the tray.

4 To make the icing, beat the egg white until frothy, then sift over the icing sugar and beat that in. Mix until smooth: you need the icing to be a thick, pipe-able paste, which holds its form rather like – and I'm sorry for the comparison – toothpaste. If it's a little thick, slacken it with just a drop of lemon juice at a time. Put this into the piping bag, and decorate the heart biscuits.

THE RAVEN'S NESTS
MAKES 4

Essential equipment
3 disposable piping bags, one
  fitted with 10mm nozzle, one
  fitted with a large star nozzle
  and one with a number
  1 writing nozzle
4 mini savarin moulds,
  greased, frozen, greased
  again then dusted with flour
Sheet of acetate/baking paper

For the cake
30g cocoa powder
100g dark muscovado sugar
50g hot water
50g Greek yoghurt
1 egg
1 tsp coffee extract (optional)
50g dark chocolate, melted in
  a heatproof bowl over a pan
  of barely simmering water
½ tsp bicarbonate of soda
50g plain flour

For the cherry mousse
2 gelatine leaves
200g pitted cherries (frozen
  are cheaper, defrost first)
80g golden caster sugar
Red food colouring
250g whipping cream

INGREDIENTS CONTINUE OVERLEAF

When I was a tot, Mum used to throw the best Halloween parties for us: bin bags torn up and hung from the doorways, cobwebs covering the entire ceiling, and even disco lights in the dining room to create an eerie environment. Bin bags, however effective in the Nineties, wouldn't quite cut it nowadays, and so I need to impress my guests with food. These little rounds of cake, filled with cherry mousse and adorned with a tempered chocolate plume of feathers, are just the thing for an adult Halloween party. They were inspired by Edgar Allan Poe's 'The Raven', that haunting poem of waiting and fear. These beautifully light chocolate, cherry and coffee cakes are well worth the wait.

1 Preheat the oven to 200°C/180°C fan/Gas 6.

2 Place the cocoa powder and sugar in a mixing bowl and stir together until well mixed and fairly lump-free. Add the hot water and stir to a smooth paste, then beat in the yoghurt, egg, extract if using, and the melted chocolate. Sift over the bicarbonate of soda and flour and fold to a smooth batter. Put the batter into the piping bag with a 10mm nozzle and divide between the 4 prepared moulds.

3 Bake for 10–14 minutes, or until a skewer gently inserted into one of the cakes comes out clean. Remove from the oven and de-mould immediately, and allow to cool on a wire rack until completely cold.

4 To make the cherry mousse, soak the gelatine leaves in a jug of cold water – put them into the water one at a time or else they'll stick together and never dissolve. Blitz the cherries to a mush in a food processor or with a stick blender, then put into a small saucepan and add the sugar. Bring the cherry pulp and sugar

THE RAVEN'S NESTS
CONTINUED

For the feather decorations
100g dark chocolate, tempered
   according to the method
   on page 13
2 tbsp cocoa powder (optional)

to a boil, then simmer and allow to reduce down to a loose compote consistency. While the cherries are still hot, squeeze the surplus moisture out of the gelatine leaves and add to the pan with the cherries. Add the food colouring. Stir until the gelatine has dissolved, then allow to cool completely, but don't let it set.

5 When the cherry compote is cool, whip the cream to soft, floppy peaks, and gently fold together with the cherry compote. Put the mousse into the piping bag fitted with the large star nozzle.

6 Place the chocolate nests on serving plates, and pipe a large, indulgent swirl of the cherry mousse in the centre of each one. Chill until needed.

7 For the tempered chocolate feather, put the tempered chocolate into the piping bag with the small writing nozzle. Pipe a fairly thick line of chocolate about 10cm long, then, with the tip of the nozzle, drag the chocolate out diagonally on either side of the line to create a feather shape. Make 12 in total, each a slightly different size, and allow to set at room temperature.

8 Once set, place 3 into the mousse of each Raven's Nest to create a dramatic, haunting finish. Sift over some cocoa powder if desired.

MINCE AND FRANGIPANE TARTLETS
MAKES 4

½ quantity Rich Sweet
  Shortcrust Pastry
  (see page 248)

For the frangipane
55g salted butter
55g golden caster sugar
1 large egg
55g ground almonds
1 tbsp plain flour
1 tsp baking powder
½ tsp almond extract
Zest of half an orange

6 tbsp best quality mincemeat
Icing sugar, to serve

Essential equipment
Four 9cm/3½-inch loose-
  bottomed tartlet tins
Disposable piping bag

Of course, no household would be complete at Christmas without a load of mince pies. I particularly love my version (well, I would, wouldn't I?); not only are they bigger than the conventional mince pie, but they come with an orangey frangipane topping. These, served with a dollop of brandy butter, will transform even the most cold-hearted Scrooge into a festive fiend.

1 Make the pastry as described on page 248, wrap in cling film and chill for at least 30 minutes.

2 Make the frangipane by creaming together the butter and sugar until light and fluffy. Then mix in the egg, almonds, flour, baking powder, almond extract and zest. Place to one side until needed.

3 Preheat the oven to 200°C/180°C fan/Gas 6.

4 Roll out the pastry on a well-floured surface to about 4mm thick. Cut out circles of pastry that are bigger than the tartlet tins. Line the tartlet tins with the pastry, pressing firmly into the grooves. Trim off any excess, and place in the freezer for 15 minutes.

5 Remove the lined tins from the freezer. Place a square of baking paper into each one, then fill with rice or baking beans. Bake on a baking sheet for 12 minutes, then remove the beans and paper, and return the tins to the oven for 10 minutes more. Remove and allow to cool slightly.

6 Spread 1½ tablespoons of mincemeat in each pastry case. Put the frangipane into the piping bag and snip off about 1cm from the end. Pipe in spirals on top of the mincemeat to cover it. Return to the oven on the baking sheet, reduce the temperature immediately to 150°C/130°C fan/Gas 2, and bake for a further 30 minutes, or until the frangipane is puffed and slightly brown around the edges.

7 Take from the oven and allow to cool completely before removing from the tins and sprinkling over a heavy snowfall of icing sugar.

GLUTEN-FREE CHOCOLATE AND HAZELNUT CELEBRATION CAKE
SERVES 12

200g dark chocolate,
  roughly chopped
300g blanched hazelnuts
150g dark muscovado sugar
150g golden caster sugar
6 eggs, separated

For the ganache
250g dark chocolate
220ml double cream
30g salted butter, softened

For the hazelnut spikes
200g golden caster sugar
About 20 blanched hazelnuts

Essential equipment
23cm/9-inch loose-bottomed
  cake tin, greased and lined
  with baking paper
Wire cooling rack
Paper clips

Is it a brownie or is it a cake? Well, it is something of sheer beauty and deliciousness anyway. The caramel-dipped hazelnuts couldn't be simpler, and they make what would otherwise look like a plain chocolate cake (not that there's anything wrong with that) into something straight out of a boutique cake store.

1 Preheat the oven to 170°C/150°C fan/Gas 3.

2 Slowly melt the chocolate in a heatproof bowl set over a pan of barely simmering water.

3 Blitz the hazelnuts in a food processor until roughly chopped, then add the sugars and blitz again to a fine sand. Pour into a mixing bowl and add the egg yolks and one white. This will be a very stiff batter, but with a bit of elbow grease – or the power of a freestanding mixer – you will cope. When well incorporated, beat in the melted chocolate and set aside.

4 Put the remaining egg whites into a clean bowl and whisk until medium peak (see page 12). Spoon a quarter of the egg white on to the thick batter and beat in to incorporate, then gently fold the remainder in. Pour into the prepared tin and bake for 35–40 minutes. A skewer inserted in the centre should come out reasonably clean, but the best indication of doneness is a smooth top with a few cracks, and a subtle springiness to the cake when gently prodded.

GLUTEN-FREE
CHOCOLATE
AND HAZELNUT
CELEBRATION
CAKE
CONTINUED

5 Remove the cake from the oven and allow to cool completely in the tin.

6 To make the ganache, place the chocolate in a heatproof bowl. Put the cream in a small saucepan and heat on high until it begins to bubble around the edges. Pour the hot cream over the chocolate and leave for 30 seconds to melt it, then, with a whisk, stir until smooth. Beat in the butter until incorporated, then pour on to a plate to cool until spreadable.

7 When the cake has cooled, remove it from the tin and place it on a cake stand or platter. Spread the ganache generously over the entire surface – as neatly or as messily as desired.

8 To make the hazelnut spikes, place a wire cooling rack on the worktop with a short side hanging over the edge by an inch. Place a sheet of baking paper on the floor directly underneath – this will catch any drops of caramel. Place a medium saucepan over a high heat and allow it to get hot. Add a quarter of the sugar and allow that to slowly melt, then add another quarter, and continue until you have used all the sugar – you may have a few lumps of sugar here and there, but the majority of it should be liquid. When the caramel turns a gorgeous amber, remove from the heat and allow to cool and thicken to the consistency of golden syrup – if it sets too solid, melt again over a low heat.

9 Take a paper clip and straighten one end – you need one end to be hooked and one end straight. Drive the straight end into one of the hazelnuts, then dredge that through the thickened caramel, coating it very generously indeed. Hook the paper clip on to the wire rack and allow the caramel to drip, like a stalactite, towards the floor and set hard. Repeat with all the hazelnuts and allow the caramel to set. When hardened, use a pair of scissors to gently snip the fine threads of caramel off the more robust, decorative spikes. Arrange the hazelnuts, spikes pointing up, in the centre of the cake.

POPPING CRANBERRY CHOCOLATE SHARDS
SERVES 2

Gold edible lustre dust
(optional but so beautiful)
300g plain or milk chocolate
150g dried cranberries
2 tbsp popping candy

Essential equipment
A4 sheet acetate (or baking
paper if you can't find this)
Baking sheet
Small paintbrush (if using
the lustre dust)

Sometimes it is the simpler things in life that are the most effective. These chocolate shards are a case of tempering chocolate, then topping it with a few bits and pieces. You'll be surprised at how much chocolatier houses sell this for when you realize how simple it is. Don't be put off by the idea of tempering: it's quite easy to master – just see page 13. With its flashes of gold lustre, this chocolate is perfect for any special occasion.

1 Place the acetate on the baking sheet and tape the ends to secure it from flapping around. If you're using the gold lustre – which you should because it looks incredible – gently paint little strips or random flashes of gold on the acetate paper.

2 Temper the chocolate according the method on page 13, and remember to make sure to test that it's ready – the most important stage of the whole process.

3 Pour the tempered chocolate on to the acetate paper, and gently move the baking sheet around to spread the chocolate out – though you don't want it too thin. While the chocolate is still melted, sprinkle over the cranberries and popping candy. Allow the chocolate to set, which should be fairly rapid. Once the chocolate is completely dry and set, gently break it up into sizeable shards, and store in an airtight container or chocolate box.

CHESTNUT AND CHOCOLATE CANDY CANE SWISS ROLL
SERVES 6–8

For the stencil paste
1 egg
25g golden caster sugar
25g plain flour
Red food colouring

For the cake batter
3 eggs
85g golden caster sugar
85g plain flour
1 tbsp sunflower oil

For the filling
200g dark chocolate,
   roughly chopped
100ml double cream
250g can sweet crème de
   marron/chestnut spread

Essential equipment
Piping bag fitted with 10mm
   nozzle
30 × 20cm/12 × 8-inch Swiss
   roll tin, greased and lined
   with baking paper

I love to have a bit of fun at Christmas with food and this candy cane roll not only tastes nothing short of awesome, but it also looks the part on the dinner table.

1 To make the paste, beat the egg with the sugar until tripled in volume, then sift in the flour and fold in with enough red gel to make a deep colour. Chill in the fridge for 30 minutes, then scrape into the piping bag. Pipe neat lines across the width of the prepared Swiss roll tin, then place in the fridge.

3 Preheat the oven to 200°C/180°C fan/Gas 6.

4 To make the cake batter, whisk the eggs in a mixing bowl with the sugar until the eggs triple in volume and reach the ribbon stage – the mixture should fall from the whisk and sit proud of the surface for 4 seconds. Sift over the flour and pour in the oil, folding in gently. When you have a smooth batter, pour it over the stencil paste, smooth the top, and bake for 10–12 minutes. It should be fairly pale, but should spring back when gently prodded. Remove from the oven and allow to cool completely.

5 To make the ganache part of the filling, place the chocolate in a heatproof bowl, and heat the cream in a small saucepan until it starts to bubble at the edges. Pour the hot cream over the chocolate and leave for 30 seconds, then whisk until smooth and glossy. Scrape on to a plate and cool until spreadable.

6 Remove the cake from the tin and place it striped-side down on a piece of clean baking paper. Spread chestnut purée over the surface, then spread on the chocolate ganache. Starting with the long edge, roll the cake up into a fairly tight spiral. Allow the ganache to set completely inside the roll before slicing to serve.

INDULGENT TREATS

Baking, whether at home or in a professional kitchen, has to be about indulgence in one way or another, for yourself or for others. Even if you are on a pernickety diet and only eating certain things, but you treat yourself to a slice of cake – even if it is a healthy cake – that is surely about mood-enhancing pleasure. You allow yourself that treat to carry you through. If I'm going to have a slice of cake – even if I am on a healthy-eating stint – I will make it count, and go for something gloriously, gorgeously, sense-satisfyingly delicious. Nothing makes you feel as good as a slice of fabulous homemade cake.

JAPANESE COTTON CHEESECAKE

SERVES 8–10

400g full-fat cream cheese
260ml milk
6 eggs, separated
85g plain flour
25g cornflour
Zest of 1 lemon
150g golden caster sugar
1 tsp vanilla bean paste
  or extract

To serve
Maple syrup
Fresh blueberries

Essential equipment
23cm/9-inch round
  springform cake tin, greased
  and lined with baking paper
  (both base and sides) and the
  outside wrapped in a double
  layer of foil
Large deep-sided roasting tray
  into which the cake tin fits

I had heard about the lightest and fluffiest cheesecake known to man, a legendary beast no humble home baker could conquer. Nonsense, said I, as I whisked egg whites into a cheesecake batter. While this cake does require caution, it really isn't difficult. Correct preparation of the cake tin helps.

1 Preheat the oven to 160°C/140°C fan/Gas 3.

2 Place the cream cheese and milk in a heatproof bowl and set over a pan of simmering water. Stir with a whisk constantly until the cream cheese has melted and you have a smooth liquid. Remove from the heat and allow to cool for 5 minutes, or until the mixture feels only warm when you test it with your finger.

3 Beat the egg yolks into the mixture, then sift over the flour and cornflour and beat that in. Pass the mixture through a sieve to remove any large lumps. Once sieved, beat in the lemon zest.

4 Place the egg whites in a mixing bowl and whisk until foamy – I do this in a freestanding electric mixer with whisk attachment. Slowly add the sugar a tablespoon at a time, while continuing to whisk. When you've put in the final addition, the mixture should be glossy, smooth and hold its shape in medium/stiff peaks – you don't want to create too stiff a meringue here as that could rise too much in the heat of the oven and cause the cheesecake to crack. Gently beat a third of the meringue into the cheese mixture, then fold in the remaining meringue, being careful not to deflate it too much, but ensuring it is well incorporated.

5 Pour the mixture gently into the prepared tin, and place in the roasting dish. Fill the roasting dish with hot water so it comes halfway up the sides of the cake tin, and bake for 1 hour 20 minutes, or until the top is a gorgeous sandy golden colour. Turn off the oven, open the door very slightly and allow the cheesecake to cool down in there for at least 90 minutes. Serve with maple syrup and fresh blueberries.

SPICED PEAR TARTE TATIN
SERVES 6

100ml water
150g golden caster sugar
1 cinnamon stick
2 cardamom pods, bruised
1 star anise
4 medium pears
40g unsalted butter, cubed
1 quantity Rough Puff Pastry
  (see page 246) or 500g shop-
  bought, all-butter puff pastry

Essential equipment
24cm/9-inch ovenproof
  frying pan

I love tarte tatin. What I especially love is the fact that you can experiment and use different fillings – or toppings, rather – and achieve some lovely flavours. This is one of my absolute favourites, and can be served at any time of the year. I love it with a dollop of Cornish ice cream.

1 Start by making a spiced caramel. Put the water, sugar, cinnamon, cardamom pods and star anise into a medium saucepan. Stir until the sugar dissolves, then set over a high heat and allow to boil away until dark golden. This usually takes about 5 minutes.

2 Meanwhile, peel the pears and cut in half lengthwise. Remove the core with a melon baller or small spoon, and put the pears into a bowl of water.

3 Once the caramel is dark golden, add the butter cubes and remove from the heat. Pour the caramel into a 24cm ovenproof frying pan. Remove the spices with tongs, saving them for later.

4 Preheat the oven to 220°C/200°C fan/Gas 7.

5 Place the pears on the caramel – being careful not to burn your fingers – hump sides down, with their fat bottoms out towards the edges of the pan.

6 Roll the pastry to about 4mm thick, and cut out a circle about 2.5cm bigger in diameter than the frying pan. Place the pastry on top of the pears and tuck it down the sides using a wooden spoon. Stab a few holes with a sharp knife, then place the frying pan in the oven and bake for 30 minutes, or until the pastry is a glorious golden brown and has puffed up.

7 To serve, remove the frying pan from the oven. Take a plate that is larger than the pan, and place it top-side down on the pan. Wearing oven gloves, or shielding your arm with a tea towel, hold the base of the plate with one hand, and with the other flip the pan over so that the tarte is pastry-side down on the plate. Decorate with the spices, and serve.

MINI UNBAKED ALASKA
MAKES 12

1 litre raspberry ice cream

For the chocolate layer
120g salted butter, softened
120g golden caster sugar
1 tsp chocolate extract
  (optional)
2 eggs
180g plain flour
40g cocoa powder

For the plain layer
120g salted butter, softened
120g golden caster sugar
1 tsp vanilla bean paste
  or extract
2 eggs
220g plain flour

For the Italian meringue
6 egg whites
340g white caster sugar
100ml water

Essential equipment
Shallow baking tray, lined
  with baking paper
30 × 20cm/12 × 8-inch Swiss
  roll tin, greased and lined
  with baking paper
7.5cm/2½-inch cookie cutter
Sugar thermometer
Piping bag fitted with
  8mm plain nozzle
Cook's blowtorch

There is something so impressive about the composition of baked Alaska, what with the cake layer, still-frozen ice cream, and baked meringue. Even though I'm promised by baker friends that a genuinely baked Alaska is easy, I'd rather cheat with my unbaked versions, using Italian meringue instead of French. These must be served within ten minutes or so of making. I just use that as an excuse to devour them without holding back. (See overleaf.)

1 Scoop out 12 portions of the ice cream, trying to get them into domes with flat bases, and place on the lined baking tray. Put into the freezer to set.

2 Preheat the oven to 210°C/190°C fan/Gas 6.

3 To make the chocolate layer, beat the butter and sugar until pale and fluffy, then beat in the chocolate extract, if using, along with the eggs. Sift over the flour and cocoa powder, then stir in to make a stiff batter. Scoop this into the prepared Swiss roll tin, and smooth it out so it fills the tin evenly.

4 Repeat step 3 to make the plain layer, then smooth this out on top of the chocolate layer. Bake for 25 minutes. Allow to cool for a minute or two, then unmould and cut out 12 discs using the cookie cutter, and set on a wire rack to cool completely. Crumble the offcuts to a rubble and put on to a large plate.

5 Take the ice cream domes from the freezer, and roll them – just the dome; not the flat base – gently in the biscuit rubble to coat them, then place them flat side down on the cake discs, and return the whole ensemble to the freezer.

6 To make the Italian meringue, place the egg whites in a mixing bowl but don't whisk just yet. (If you have a freestanding electric mixer with whisk attachment, do use that. Otherwise you'll need some help here. Someone to hold the electric whisk while you pour the sugar syrup, for example.) Mix the sugar and water together in a medium saucepan and set over a high heat. Allow to boil until the mixture reaches 110°C on the thermometer. When it does, start whisking the eggs on medium until they are foamy, then, when the sugar syrup reaches 118°C, remove the pan from the heat and with the whisk on medium, slowly pour the syrup down the side of the bowl and into the egg whites. Turn up the speed to full and whisk until very stiff and the meringue is at room temperature – 5–7 minutes. Scoop this into the piping bag.

7 Take the ice cream from the freezer. Pipe meringue spikes to cover the entire surface of the ice cream, leaving the biscuit edges bare – rather like an albino hedgehog. With the cook's blowtorch, lightly char the spikes of meringue. Serve immediately.

ROSE SWIRL ANGEL FOOD CAKE
SERVES 10–12

300g egg white
1 tsp vanilla bean paste
 or extract
300g golden caster sugar
100g plain flour (use extra fine
 cake flour if you can find it)
Zest of 1 large lemon

For the buttercream
400g unsalted butter, softened
800g icing sugar
2 tbsp milk
1 tsp vanilla bean paste
 or extract
Pearlescent icing balls,
 to decorate

Essential equipment
23cm/9-inch angel food
 cake tin, ungreased
Disposable piping bag fitted
 with large star nozzle

This cake is stunning. The pale, light texture is just out of this world, and the soft swirled icing is a real centrepiece and a perfectly – though light – indulgent treat. The key to the sharp swirls is to ensure that the buttercream is whipped well so that it isn't overly stiff, but nor should it be so soft that it droops out of shape. An angel food cake tin is round with a tube in the middle – the shape that best supports such delicate batter – and feet that enable you to invert it easily. Weighing the egg whites gives you a much surer result.

1 Preheat the oven to 170°C/150°C fan/Gas 3.

2 Place the egg whites and vanilla in a clean mixing bowl – a freestanding electric mixer with whisk attachment if you have one. Sift half of the sugar with the flour into another mixing bowl and add the lemon zest, then place the remaining sugar in a small bowl. Beat the egg whites to just stiff peaks, then, as you continuously whisk the eggs, slowly add the sugar to create a glossy, shiny meringue which holds its shape in stiff peaks. Scoop this mixture on top of the flour and sugar and, with a thin spatula or large metal spoon, gently fold the floury sugar into the meringue, being extremely careful not to deflate it.

3 Gently pour the mixture into the cake tin, and level it off with a spoon or palette knife. Bake for 40–45 minutes, or until a skewer inserted into the centre of the cake comes out clean. Remove from the oven and invert the cake tin. (Rest the central tube on a can of beans if your tin doesn't have the little feet to support it.) Allow it to cool like this for at least 2 hours.

4 To make the buttercream, whisk the butter until it is very pale and fluffy – about 5 minutes using a

ROSE SWIRL ANGEL FOOD CAKE CONTINUED

handheld electric mixer, or 3 minutes in a freestanding electric mixer with whisk attachment. Then add the icing sugar, and gently mix together with a wooden spoon to avoid the icing sugar creating a sweet cloud in the kitchen. Add the milk and vanilla and whisk again for at least 7 minutes, or until the mixture is very pale – almost white – and very soft.

5 Pile the buttercream into the piping bag. With the cake turned out on to a plate or cake stand, start at the top of the cake and pipe a little, tight swirl of buttercream, like a rose. Pipe another swirl/rose next to that, then another, and so on, then repeat one line below this, and repeat until the cake is covered in buttercream roses. Inside the ring of the cake, simply pipe lines of buttercream from the bottom to the top.

6 To finish, place a pearlescent icing ball in the centre of each rose swirl.

CINNAMON CARAMEL TUILES
MAKES 8

For the tuile biscuits
100g unsalted butter
100g plain flour
100g icing sugar
1–2 tsp ground cinnamon
100g egg whites

For the caramel filling
75g sugar
30g unsalted butter
20ml double cream

Essential equipment
2 baking sheets, greased

Indulgence could not be manifested in a more perfect form. These crispy and chewy creatures are nothing short of divine, and are guaranteed to vanish soon after being made. Cinnamon is my spice of choice for these.

1 Melt the butter in a medium saucepan over a low heat, but don't allow to boil. Once melted, remove from the heat and allow to cool slightly.

2 Sift the flour, icing sugar and cinnamon into a mixing bowl to blend together. Make a well in the centre of the floury mound, and add the egg whites and the cooled, melted butter. Whisk together until you have a thick, smooth paste. Place in the fridge to firm up for at least an hour.

3 Preheat the oven to 200°C/180°C fan/Gas 6.

4 Blob 16 teaspoonfuls of the mixture on to the baking sheets, making sure they are well spaced apart as the tuiles will spread as they bake – you will probably need to do this in batches. Bake for 8–12 minutes, or until the tuiles are a gorgeous golden brown on top, and a little darker around the edges – these need to be crispy. Remove from the oven and allow to cool on the baking sheet for a few minutes, before transferring to a wire rack to finish cooling.

5 To make the caramel filling, heat a medium saucepan over a medium-high heat. Sprinkle a third of the sugar into the saucepan and allow it to melt in the heat of the pan. Once most of the sugar has melted, add another third and gently stir this into the melted sugar. Repeat with the remaining third, and then allow the melted sugar to turn a golden amber colour. Once this colour is achieved, quickly but carefully add the butter and cream – it will spatter a little – and whisk in until you have a smooth caramel. Spoon a blob of this filling on to 8 of the tuiles – on to the flat sides – and then top with the remaining 8 tuiles to make biscuity sandwiches.

FALLEN ANGEL CAKE SERVES 10–12

300g egg whites
1 tsp vanilla bean paste
  or extract
300g golden caster sugar
100g plain flour (use extra
  fine cake flour, if you have it)
2 tbsp cocoa powder

For the sinful boozy drizzle
100g raspberries
  (frozen will do)
100ml water
1 tbsp orange liqueur

For the buttercream
250g unsalted butter, softened
370g icing sugar
1 tbsp milk

Essential equipment
1 × 23cm/9-inch angel food
  cake tin, ungreased

Angel food cake has to be the palest, lightest cake there is. I wanted to make this a little more exciting, though, so this is a layer of angelic white cake, then one of devilish chocolate angel cake, topped with a fluffy, cloud-like buttercream, which is then 'fallen' by virtue of the boozy, raspberry drizzle. If you are making this for children to eat, simply leave the booze out. It will be less 'fallen', but just as sinfully scrumptious. On another advisory note, I really do hate being so pernickety by weighing egg whites, but because this recipe is a delicate ratio, I strongly advise that you do.

1 Preheat the oven to 170°C/150°C fan/Gas 3.

2 Place the egg whites and vanilla in a clean mixing bowl – a freestanding electric mixer with whisk attachment if you have one. Sift half of the sugar with the flour into another mixing bowl, then place the remaining half of sugar into a small bowl. Beat the egg whites to just stiff peaks, then, as you continuously whisk the eggs, slowly add the sugar to create a glossy, shiny meringue, which holds its shape in stiff peaks. Scoop this mixture on top of the flour and sugar, and with a thin spatula or large metal spoon, gently fold the floury sugar into the meringue, being extremely careful not to deflate the meringue. Then, scoop half of this back into the original meringue mixing bowl, and sift over the cocoa powder, and fold that in too.

3 Gently scoop the plain mixture into the ungreased cake tin, level it off with a spoon, then scoop the chocolate mixture on top of that, levelling it off. Bake for 40–45 minutes, or until a skewer inserted into

FALLEN ANGEL CAKE CONTINUED

the centre of the cake comes out clean. Remove from the oven and invert the cake tin, resting the centre of the cake tin on a can of beans so that the cake isn't touching anything. Allow it to cool like this for at least 2 hours.

4 Make the drizzle. Heat together the raspberries and water until the raspberries just lose their shape. Remove from the heat and stir in the orange liqueur if using. Pass through a sieve to remove the seeds.

5 Make the buttercream by beating the butter with a whisk – freestanding electric or handheld – until it is pale and fluffy. Then add the icing sugar and milk and whisk for a good five minutes, or until the buttercream is very pale.

6 When the cake has cooled, gently run a knife in between the cake and tin, and turn the cake out on to a cake stand. Cover the entire cake in buttercream, making tiny peaks with a palette knife, then drizzle over the sinful sauce.

GUINNESS AND BLACK BATTENBERG
SERVES 6–8

45g salted butter, softened
100g dark muscovado sugar
45g golden caster sugar
90g Greek yoghurt
2 small eggs
120g self-raising flour
30g cocoa powder
½ tsp bicarbonate of soda
150g Guinness (I weigh this
　rather than measure as
　the froth can impede an
　accurate measurement)

For the filling
100g blackberries
60g golden caster sugar
Zest of 1 lemon
Juice of ½ lemon
2 tbsp crème de cassis
　liqueur (optional)

For the wrap
600g ready-to-roll fondant icing
Black food colouring

To serve
Fondant roses (optional)

Essential equipment
20 × 15cm/8 × 6-inch
　battenberg tin, greased and
　floured to prevent sticking
Cocktail stick

The first sip of alcohol I had was out of my father's pint of Guinness and blackcurrant. I remember vividly how we were in a pub enjoying a Sunday lunch, and I loved the way the froth of Guinness sat on his upper lip like a milky moustache. The flavour of the alluring black drink was, even for a child, so beautiful – the perfect balance of sweet currant and burned stout, though I don't imagine I would have described it like that back then. This battenberg is a dramatic showpiece.

1 Preheat the oven to 180°C/160°C fan/Gas 4.

2 Beat the butter and sugars together in a mixing bowl – either with a wooden spoon, handheld electric whisk or freestanding mixer and paddle attachment – until the sugar is well dissolved and the mixture is fluffy. Beat in the yoghurt and eggs. Sift together the flour, cocoa powder and bicarbonate of soda, and fold in until well incorporated. Pour over the Guinness and fold in until just amalgamated. Divide between the sections of the tin, and bake for 15–20 minutes, or until a skewer inserted into the centre comes out completely clean. Remove from the oven and allow to cool in the tin until cold.

3 While the cake bakes, make the jam filling. Put the blackberries in a medium saucepan with the sugar, lemon zest and juice and bring to the boil, stir, then reduce to a rapid simmer and allow to thicken until it reaches the thread stage: take a little bit of jam on a spoon and put a small amount between forefinger and thumb as you open and close them. If a thread of jam is formed, it's ready.

Remove it from the heat and stir in the cassis, if using. Allow to cool completely.

4 To assemble, trim the tops of the cakes to flatten them if they domed over the edges of the tin while in the oven. Spread the jam over the long sides of each strip of cake that will meet, reserving a little jam for later. Stack them together evenly. Refrigerate to firm up while you prepare the icing.

5 To colour the icing, knead the fondant a little to soften it, then add a dab of colour – a cocktail stick is best. Knead the colour in – you may want to wear rubber gloves for this. Add more colouring until you have the desired depth of black. Roll the fondant icing out on a board dusted with plenty of cornflour (icing sugar makes fondant icing crack) – you need it to be long enough to cover the length of the cake, and wide enough to wrap around it, with a little spare just in case. I find using two lengths of string to be the easiest way to measure it.

6 Retrieve the cake from the fridge and spread the remaining jam over the sides. With the short edge of the fondant closest to you, place the cake horizontally on to the icing. Roll the cake up the icing, taking the icing with it. When you get to the icing join, trim the surplus icing and make it look as neat as possible. Turn it round so that the seam of the icing is on the bottom. With a sharp serrated knife, trim the ends to neaten and expose the black bricks of cake.

CHOCOLATE MARBLE TART
SERVES 6–8

1 quantity Chocolate Rough
   Puff Pastry (see page 247)
200g dark chocolate,
   roughly chopped
200g white chocolate,
   roughly chopped
400ml double cream
2 eggs

Essential equipment
Baking sheet
25cm/10-inch loose-
   bottomed flan tin

You'd think a double serving of chocolate would be more than enough, but no, I like to push things to the limit, and so not only does this include a chocolate pastry, but a chocolate rough puff pastry. Actually, bold assertions of indulgence aside, the flakiness of the pastry in this means that the tart itself isn't overfacing. The gentle sporadic flake, with the creamy, set chocolate, makes for a glorious result.

1 Preheat the oven to 200°C/180°C fan/Gas 6 and slide the baking sheet into the oven to heat up.

2 Roll out the rough puff pastry on a well-floured surface and use it to line the flan tin. Prick the base with a fork and freeze for 10 minutes. Line with baking paper, fill with baking beans or rice and bake on the hot sheet for 15 minutes. Remove the paper and beans and bake for a further 10 minutes – keep an eye on it and flatten the pastry down if it starts to blister. Remove from the oven and allow to cool.

3 Reduce the oven to 160°C/140°C fan/Gas 3.

4 Put the dark chocolate in one heatproof bowl, and the white chocolate in another. Put the cream in a medium saucepan and heat on high until it starts to bubble around the edges, then pour half over each chocolate. Leave for just a minute before whisking each until smooth and glossy. Allow to cool for a few minutes, and then beat an egg into each ganache.

5 To fill the tart shell, pour the ganaches into the shell at the same time, swirling them around to create a marble effect. Bake for 15–20 minutes, or until the filling is set with a slight tremble in the centre when the tart is moved. Cool before serving.

GLUTEN-FREE PISTACHIO AND CHOCOLATE TORTE
SERVES 8–10

6 large eggs, separated
150g pistachio kernels,
  unsalted and de-shelled
120g ground almonds
30g cocoa powder
1 tsp gluten-free
  baking powder
150g golden caster sugar
150g light muscovado sugar

For the topping
100g milk chocolate
100g white chocolate

Essential equipment
23cm/9-inch loose-bottomed
  round cake tin, greased, the
  base lined with baking paper

Gluten intolerance seems to be becoming more and more common. In my eyes, though, that is no reason not to enjoy home-baked goodies. This torte is spectacular, and really hits the sweet spot. Due to the large amount of nuts in this, it does keep well, and is probably even better the day after it is made.

1 Preheat the oven to 170°C/150°C fan/Gas 3.

2 Place the egg yolks and one white into a large mixing bowl, and the remaining whites into another. Put the pistachios, ground almonds, cocoa powder, baking powder and sugars into a food processor and blitz into a fine powder. Pour this powder into the bowl with the egg yolks and beat together – this will be very thick indeed but don't give up.

3 In the other mixing bowl, whisk the egg whites until stiff peaks form. Gently scoop these on top of the other mixture, and fold together extremely carefully – you will need a bit of elbow grease, but try not to deflate the egg whites.

4 When well incorporated, pour this into the prepared baking tin. Bake for 40–50 minutes, or until the torte gently springs back when lightly touched. Allow to cool for 5 minutes, before turning out from the tin and resting on a wire rack until completely cool.

5 To finish, melt the chocolates separately – the best way is in heatproof bowls over pans of barely simmering water. Drizzle them randomly over the torte to create a messy, chocolatey pattern.

BOOZY BRAMBLEBERRY, HONEY AND OATMEAL MERINGUE MESSES

MAKES 4

For the meringues
4 egg whites
225g golden caster sugar
60g medium oatmeal
60g blackberries

For the topping
200g blackberries,
   plus extra to serve
70g honey
25ml bourbon
400ml double cream
1 tbsp icing sugar
1 tsp vanilla bean paste
   or extract

Essential equipment
Baking sheet lined with
   baking paper

Indulgence doesn't need to be rich, chocolaty and buttery. It can just as easily be something light and pillowy. I adore pavlova as it is, but the added touches of oatmeal and honey make it divine. (See overleaf.)

1 Preheat the oven to 140°C/120°C fan/Gas 1.

2 Place the egg whites and caster sugar in a heatproof bowl and set over a pan of barely simmering water. Whisk until the mixture feels a little hot to the touch – though whisk constantly to avoid it scrambling – then remove from the heat and whisk until very thick and stiff. Use a handheld electric whisk, or pour it into a freestanding mixer with whisk attachment and use that – it will take 5–7 minutes to reach very stiff peaks. Add the oatmeal and blackberries to the bowl, and fold until the oatmeal is well incorporated – don't knock any air out of the meringue.

3 Using a large metal spoon, scoop four blobs of meringue on to the baking sheet. Slide into the oven, reduce the heat to 120°C/100°C fan/Gas ¼, and bake for 25 minutes, then turn off the oven and open the door slightly. Allow to cool in the oven, then remove.

4 To make the topping, place the blackberries and honey in a small saucepan and bring to the boil, stirring occasionally. When thick but still with lumps of blackberry, remove from the heat and stir in the bourbon. Allow to cool.

5 Whip the double cream with the icing sugar and vanilla to soft, floppy peaks.

6 To assemble, simply take a meringue and drape over the soft, pillowy cream, then drizzle over some of the sauce. Scatter over a few blackberries and serve, 1 or 2 per person, depending on greed.

MY VERSION OF DOUGHSANTS MAKES 10–12

1 quantity Rough Puff Danish
   Pastry (see page 248)
100g white or golden
   caster sugar
Sunflower oil, for frying

For the icing
100g icing sugar
1 tsp orange juice

Essential equipment
9cm/3½-inch round
   cookie cutter
5cm/2-inch round
   cookie cutter
Large baking sheet, greased
Large carrier bag or bin bag
Deep-fat fryer or large
   saucepan and sugar
   thermometer

The 'cronut' craze hit us in spring 2013, and at first I sat there thinking it was an abhorrent-sounding delicacy. Then I considered it, and my mouth watered, so I tried it. I'm glad I did, because these really are the foodstuffs of fallen angels. This is my take on the doughnut–croissant cross. Fill them with whatever you like. I love them with lemon curd and cream. And in the interests of 'waste not want not': instead of throwing away the centre discs of pastry from the doughsants, why not allow them to prove, fry in oil for just a minute or two on each side, dredge in sugar, and you have 'creignets' – croissant-dough beignets.

1 Flour the worktop and rolling pin, roll out the pastry to roughly 45 × 35cm, then trim to a neat 40 × 30cm. Cut out 10 rounds using the larger cookie cutter, then cut out circles using the smaller cutter – so you have rings of Danish pastry. Place these on the baking sheet and cover with the carrier bag or bin bag. Allow to prove until swollen: between 1 and 3 hours.

2 Sprinkle the caster sugar on a plate.

3 When the dough rings have swollen, pour sunflower oil into the deep-fat fryer, or enough sunflower oil into a saucepan so that it is at least 8cm deep. Heat the oil to 170°C. Drop three or four doughsants into the oil, and fry for about 2 minutes on each side or until a lovely golden brown. Dredge each fried doughsant in the caster sugar, then arrange on a wire rack to cool.

4 Make the topping by beating together the icing sugar and orange juice until the icing is pourable but holds its shape – you may need to adjust the icing sugar or orange juice to achieve this consistency. Spoon the topping over the doughsants, and serve immediately.

FENNEL TEA TRUFFLES
MAKES 20–24

250g plain chocolate, chips
  or roughly chopped bars
125ml freshly boiled water
2 fennel tea bags
1 heaped teaspoon edible
  gold lustre powder
  (optional but beautiful)
100g cocoa powder

Essential equipment
Disposable piping bag fitted
  with large star nozzle
Baking sheet, very
  lightly greased

Homemade chocolates are really rather rewarding, and if you can bear to part with these flavoursome logs, then as a gift they are sure to please the recipient. I normally store these in an airtight container at a low room temperature, but if your house is on the hot side, pop the container in the fridge.

1 Place the chocolate in a heatproof bowl and set to one side. Put the boiled water and tea bags into a jug and allow to infuse for about 10 minutes. After this time, remove the tea bags and rewarm the water – you don't want it to be boiling, but hot enough that you can't hold your finger in it. Pour it on to the chocolate and let the chocolate slowly melt for just a minute, then, using a small whisk, bring the chocolate and the tea together until you have a smooth, glossy ganache. Spread this on a plate and allow to thicken; depending on the temperature of the room, this could take 1–2 hours, but don't put it into the fridge.

2 Keep an eye on the ganache and when it is the consistency of a chocolate spread, scrape it into the piping bag and pipe long straight lines along the baking sheet – as long as the baking sheet. Put the baking sheet into the fridge and allow the ganache to set until firm – a good hour should do the trick.

3 If you're using the lustre, sift together the lustre and cocoa powder on to another plate; otherwise, just sift the cocoa powder. Remove the chocolate from the fridge. Heat a sharp knife by dipping it into a jug of hot water, and use it to cut small, evenly sized truffles from the chocolate lines. Roll these, quickly to avoid them melting, in the cocoa powder. Store as recommended above.

UTTERLY NUTTERLY SHORTBREADS
MAKES 16–20

For the shortbread base
110g golden caster sugar
225g salted butter, at room temperature
Seeds from 1 vanilla pod, or 1 tsp vanilla paste or extract
340g plain flour

For the topping
500g golden caster sugar
100ml water
160g salted butter, in 1cm cubes
200ml double cream
150g pecans, roughly chopped
150g hazelnuts, roughly chopped
100g dried apricots, roughly chopped

To finish
100g dark chocolate, roughly chopped

Essential equipment
Deep-sided 20 × 25cm/ 8 × 10-inch baking tray, lined with baking paper

With a buttery shortbread base and chewy, nutty topping, these little bites are indulgence in true, tangible form. I make these in advance and store them in an airtight container to dip into when I've earned a treat – though I must be an angel, as I'm constantly chewing on one of these!

1 Preheat the oven to 180°C/160°C fan/Gas 4.

2 To make the shortbread, cream the sugar and butter together along with the vanilla. When light and fluffy, sift in the flour and mix into a firm dough. Press this into the base of the baking tray, prick all over with a fork, then refrigerate for 10 minutes. Bake for 15–20 minutes or until a pale golden colour. Allow to cool.

3 To make the caramel, stir the sugar and water together in a saucepan, then place over a high heat and allow to go a dark amber colour without stirring it again – this will take up to 15 minutes, but keep an eye on it as it can turn very quickly. When it goes amber, reduce the heat to medium and stir in the butter and cream (be careful, as it will spit ferociously). Use a balloon whisk to beat together for a few minutes, or until smooth and light, then remove from the heat. Pour in the nuts and fruit and stir until each nut is coated. Tip this on top of the shortbread and smooth out as neatly as possible. Allow to set – it will be very chewy and you will just be able to get your knife through. When set, slice into 16–20 pieces.

4 To finish, place the chopped chocolate into a heatproof bowl and set over a pan of barely simmering water. Allow the chocolate to melt, then drizzle it liberally over the slices of shortbread.

MONT BLANC BISCUIT BUTTIES
MAKES 16–18

200g dark chocolate,
  roughly chopped
20g unsalted butter
2 eggs
100g dark muscovado sugar
70g light muscovado sugar
80g plain flour
½ tsp baking powder
¼ tsp salt

For the marshmallow filling
3 gelatine leaves
200g golden caster sugar
75g golden syrup
100ml water
1 × 250g sweet crème de
  marron/chestnut spread

Essential equipment
At least 2 baking sheets,
  lined with baking paper
Sugar or digital food
  thermometer
Disposable piping bag, with a
  little of the end snipped off

The only thing better than chestnut purée is a chocolate, marshmallow and chestnut purée combo, all together in one indulgent biscuit butty.

1 Preheat the oven to 200°C/180°C fan/Gas 6. Place the chocolate and butter into a heatproof bowl over a pan of barely simmering water, and allow to melt slowly. Meanwhile, whisk together the eggs and sugars until well combined. Beat the melted chocolate and butter into the sugar and egg, then sift over the flour, baking powder and salt, and beat to a smooth, glossy batter. Allow to cool and thicken slightly.

2 Scoop heaped teaspoons of the batter on to the lined baking sheets, well apart as they will spread in the oven. You should end up with about 36 blobs, so you might need to bake in batches. Bake for 10–12 minutes, or until well risen, shiny, and cracked over the surface. Allow to cool, out of the oven, on the baking sheet, before removing with a palette knife.

3 To make the filling, submerge the gelatine leaves, one by one, in a bowl of cold water. Place the sugar, syrup and water in a medium saucepan and heat on high until it reaches 118°C. Quickly squeeze the excess moisture from the gelatine, add to the pan and swirl to dissolve. Pour this into a freestanding electric mixer and whisk on full speed until very thick, sticky and only slightly warm: about 5 minutes. (Takes about 10 minutes using a handheld electric whisk.)

4 Turn half the cookies over so they are bottom up. Spoon a teaspoon of chestnut purée on to each. Pile the marshmallow into the piping bag, then pipe a ring of marshmallow around the chestnut purée. Sandwich the remaining cookies on top.

ROCHER POPS
MAKES 18–20

80g salted butter
100g Nutella
2 eggs
100g flour
½ tsp bicarbonate of soda
75g golden caster sugar

For the ganache covering
200g dark chocolate,
 roughly chopped
100g milk chocolate,
 roughly chopped
200ml double cream

For the hazelnut covering
200g skinless hazelnuts, finely
 chopped but not pulverized
Gold leaf, to decorate

Essential equipment
Disposable piping bag with
 end snipped off
12-hole cake pop mould,
 well greased

*I swore I would never bake a cake pop in my life –
I just don't see the attraction with baking fads. I was,
however, given a gorgeous cake pop tin, and so I had to
use it. Rather than making typical garish, claggy pops
from old cake crumbs and a load of old buttercream,
I make mine freshly baked using a special mould.
Silicone moulds are available but I find the metal
ones much more reliable. These are gorgeous as
dinner party treats, or for cold, dark winter nights.*

1 Preheat the oven to 200°C/180°C fan/Gas 6.

2 Beat all the ingredients together into a smooth
batter, scoop into the piping bag and pipe into one
half of the cake pop mould, filling the half sphere
well. Pop the other half of the mould in place, then
bake for 7–8 minutes. Remove from the oven and
allow to cool completely. Repeat with the remaining
batter and the cooled, re-greased mould.

3 Make the ganache by placing the chopped chocolates
into a heatproof bowl. Heat the cream in a medium
saucepan over a high heat until it just starts to bubble
around the edges, pour on to the chocolate and leave it
for about 30 seconds. Using a whisk, mix to a smooth,
glossy ganache.

4 Sprinkle the chopped hazelnuts on to a plate. Dip
each cake pop into the ganache to cover it well, then
roll in the hazelnuts. Allow the ganache to set for a
good hour, then place a little gold leaf on to each pop.

COOKIE DOUGH FUDGE

MAKES 25–30 PIECES

For the cookie dough
75g unsalted butter, softened
40g golden caster sugar
40g light muscovado sugar
1 tsp vanilla bean paste
   or extract
1 tsp golden syrup
125g plain flour
75g dark chocolate chips

For the fudge
150ml whole milk
150ml double cream
250g golden caster sugar
100g light brown soft sugar
100g unsalted butter, cubed
1/8 tsp table salt

Essential equipment
Baking sheet
Sugar or digital food
   thermometer
20cm/8-inch square cake tin,
   greased and lined with
   baking paper

I never used to like fudge, until I made my own. This is a gorgeous thing to make, not only because it tastes so sensationally satisfying, but also because the process itself is nothing short of lovely – stirring together cream, butter and sugar is the work of angels. Once this is set and cut, it should be stored in an airtight container at room temperature.

1 Make the cookie dough by placing the butter and sugars in a mixing bowl and beating until pale and fluffy. Beat in the vanilla and golden syrup, before mixing in the flour and chocolate chips to create fairly stiff dough. Divide this into about 25 little balls, then set on a baking sheet and place in the freezer for a good 30 minutes.

2 Make the fudge by placing the milk, cream, sugars and butter in a medium saucepan. Heat on medium until the butter melts, stirring occasionally, then bring to the boil and allow to bubble for about 15 minutes. When the fudge reaches 118°C on the thermometer, remove from the heat and stir in the salt, then allow to cool slightly, before mixing again until the shine starts to subside. Pour this into the prepared tin and allow to cool until room temperature, then dot in the frozen cookie dough balls evenly. Allow this to set, but don't put it into the fridge because it will oxidize and sweat.

3 Once the fudge has set, cut into about 25 chunks.

CHOCOLATE MUD MUG PUD
SERVES 1

Ingredients per person
55g salted butter, softened
55g light muscovado sugar
½ tsp vanilla bean paste
   or extract
1 medium egg
45g plain flour
10g cocoa powder
½ tsp baking powder
30g chocolate chips
   (dark, milk or white)

I love to bake, that is no secret, but sometimes I just haven't the energy to be slogging about the kitchen, or the patience to be waiting for something in the oven. I often have a craving for something sweet, but don't necessarily want to wait for three-quarters of an hour while it bakes. So this pudding is the result of my impatience. Once these are baked – or, should I say, microwaved – you can turn them out of the mug on to a plate, but I prefer to scoop a dollop of ice cream on top of mine and devour it from the mug.

1 If you have a food processor, place the ingredients, except the chocolate chips, into it and blitz into a smooth batter. Then fold in the chocolate chips, before scooping the mixture into a mug – and I mean mug, no dainty teacups here please. Place into the microwave, set to medium power and heat for 3–4 minutes, or until the sponge is perfectly baked through.

2 If you don't have a food processor, beat the butter and sugar until fluffy, then beat in the remaining ingredients – don't bother with any fancy folding, you want this to be pudding-like – and bake as above.

HOT TODDY SPONGE PUDDINGS
MAKES 4

For the whisky
*   butterscotch sauce*
150g golden caster sugar
150ml double cream
150ml whisky

For the sponge puddings
115g salted butter, softened
75g golden caster sugar
40g runny honey
Zest of 1 large lemon
2 eggs
115g self-raising flour

Essential equipment
4 × 180ml/16fl oz pudding
    moulds, greased with butter

In the depths of winter, I seek comfort. Be it a roaring log fire, a mug of hot mulled wine or even a pub supper, I am constantly on the search for warmth and cosiness. These puddings are perfect. Even better would be to eat them in front of a roaring log fire with a mug of hot mulled wine on the side – a winter wonderland in the making. This is particularly incredible served with a lemon or salted caramel ice cream.

1 To make the sauce, place the sugar in a large saucepan over a high heat. Allow the sugar to melt, swirling – not stirring – the pan constantly. This prevents the sugar from caramelizing unevenly. When the sugar has molten and is a glorious, golden brown, dribble in the cream a little at a time, stirring constantly – this will spit at you violently; just lean back and stir. When the cream is well incorporated, add the whisky and stir that in too, until the mixture just bubbles. You want to burn off the majority of the alcohol but you don't want to lose that glorious whisky flavour, so as soon as it bubbles, take it off the heat. Set to one side until needed.

2 Preheat the oven to 180°C/160°C fan/Gas 4.

3 Make the sponge by beating together the butter and sugar until pale and fluffy – you can do this in a freestanding mixer fitted with a paddle attachment. Add the honey and lemon zest, incorporating well, then beat in the eggs. Sift the flour over and fold it in.

4 Spoon 2 tablespoons of the whisky sauce into the base of each pudding mould – saving the rest for serving – then divide the pudding batter between the moulds. Place on a baking tray and bake for 20–30 minutes, or until well risen and a skewer inserted into the centre comes out reasonably clean. Because of the whisky sauce, the skewer may be moist, but anything attached to it needs to be baked, so keep in the oven a little longer in that case.

5 Turn out on to plates or into bowls, and serve with a boozy drizzle of the remaining whisky syrup.

SIMPLE ESSENTIALS

These are the backbone recipes used throughout this book. I hope, and expect, that you will treat this book disgustingly. I want there to be pen marks all over the pages, bits of cake batter sticking pages together, pastry fingerprints everywhere. A recipe book that isn't abused is like Christmas with no fairy lights, or a Friday night without a bottle of wine and a bag of frozen gummi bears – or is that just me? These basic recipes are not only for the bakes in this book, they are also here as staples for you to experiment with and create your own bakes with. Use the book as good practice, then spread your baking wings!

CHOUX PASTRY
MAKES ABOUT 600G

Ingredients for 1 quantity
220ml water
80g unsalted butter
Pinch of salt
Generous pinch of sugar
125g plain flour
220g beaten egg

Ingredients for ½ quantity
110ml water
40g unsalted butter
Pinch of salt
Pinch of sugar
65g plain flour
110g beaten egg

This pastry is easy to make and gives spectacular results.

1 In a medium saucepan, gently heat the water, butter, salt and sugar until just boiling and the butter has melted.

2 Pour in the flour and beat vigorously with a wooden spoon until the paste is smooth and comes away from the sides. This should be done over the heat, but make sure you keep the paste moving so it doesn't burn. Decant into a cold bowl, and allow to cool for about 5 minutes.

3 Add the beaten egg, a little at a time, and incorporate well. This does take a while, and the mixture may look split at first but it will come together. You need to get the paste to 'dropping' consistency. That is, when you scoop up a large amount, it should drop back down into the bowl within 5 seconds.

4 When the pastry is ready, put it into a piping bag for use. It will not keep and should be used straight away.

ROUGH PUFF PASTRY
MAKES ABOUT 600G

250g plain flour, plus extra for dusting
250g salted butter, in 2cm cubes
1 tsp lemon juice
125–150ml cold water

A rough puff, in my opinion, gives just as good a 'puff' as a full puff pastry, and is a little less demanding to make. Of course, it still takes practice and patience, but where would we be without those two blessings?

1 Put the flour and butter in a large mixing bowl and gently rub some of the butter through the flour – you still need large chunks of butter.

2 Stir the lemon juice into the water, then add to the flour, a little at a time, using your hands to bring the ingredients together. Tip out on to the worktop and lightly press and roll the pastry into a scraggy ball.

3 Flour the worktop and a rolling pin. Roll the pastry out into a long thin rectangle – about 12cm wide, and as long as it becomes when about 1cm thick. Brush excess flour from the pastry with a pastry brush. Fold the two ends so they meet in the centre; brush excess flour off, then fold these doubled-up ends together like a book (this is called the 'book fold'.) Turn the dough a quarter turn and roll it away from you into a long rectangle again. Fold again as above, then wrap in baking paper and chill in the fridge for 15 minutes.

4 Remove from the fridge, repeat the rolling and book fold twice, making sure always to start with the folded edges of the pastry vertical, and to roll away from you. Chill the pastry until you are ready to use it.

CHOCOLATE ROUGH PUFF PASTRY
MAKES ABOUT 600G

230g plain flour, plus extra for dusting
1 tsp table salt
20g cocoa powder
250g unsalted butter, cut into 2cm cubes, fridge cold
125–140ml ice-cold water

Who could resist a pastry with layers of buttery, crispy flakes and flavoured with chocolate? If you have mastered rough puff, then have a go at this. I created this pastry for my Chocolate Marble Tart on page 227.

1 Sift the flour, salt and cocoa powder into a large bowl, and add the butter. Gently rub some of the butter through the flour – you still need large chunks of butter.

2 Add the water to the mixture, a little at a time, using your hands to bring the ingredients together. Tip out on to the worktop and lightly press and roll the pastry into a scraggy ball.

3 Flour the worktop and a rolling pin. Roll the pastry out into a long thin rectangle – about 12cm wide, and as long as it becomes when about 1cm thick. Brush excess flour from the pastry with a pastry brush. Fold the two ends so they meet in the centre; brush excess flour off, then fold these doubled-up ends together like a book (this is called the 'book fold'.) Turn the dough a quarter turn and roll it away from you into a long rectangle again. Fold again as above, then wrap in baking paper and chill in the fridge for 15 minutes.

4 Remove from the fridge, repeat the rolling and book fold twice, making sure always to start with the folded edges of the pastry vertical, and to roll away from you. Chill the pastry until you are ready to use it.

SHORTCRUST PASTRY
MAKES ABOUT 450G

250g plain flour
125g salted butter, in 1cm cubes
1 egg
Cold water

The most basic of the pastries: buttery, flaky and perfect for savoury and sweet bakes.

1 Place the flour and butter in a bowl, and swiftly but gently rub the butter into the flour until the mixture resembles fine crumbs with some pea-sized lumps of butter.

2 Beat the egg in a cup, then add to the flour along with a teaspoon of cold water. Using your hands, gently clump the mixture together. If necessary, add more water, a teaspoon at a time, until the mixture comes together well, then gently knead it, though only for a second.

3 Wrap in baking paper and chill in the fridge for at least 30 minutes before using.

TIP
If you have a food processor, put the flour and butter in it and use the blade attachment to pulse until the butter is in small pea-sized lumps. Add the egg and a little water and blitz, adding more water a teaspoon at a time if necessary, until the dough comes together into a ball. Remove and continue as above.

ROUGH PUFF DANISH PASTRY
MAKES ABOUT 600G

90ml water
90ml milk
300g white bread flour, plus extra for dusting
7g fast-action yeast
5g salt
20g sugar
250g unsalted butter, cut into 2cm cubes, fridge cold

There is little more satisfying to the home baker than a batch of homemade croissants, or something made successfully with Danish pastry. The regular method of making Danish though – akin to making true puff pastry – is dull, tedious, and extremely difficult to get quite right, in my opinion. I treat my Danish pastry as I treat my puff pastry: rough. This dough freezes well for up to 3 months. Make to the end of step 4, then freeze. Defrost overnight in a fridge, then continue as the recipe requires.

1 Put the water and milk in a jug and chill in the fridge until required.

2 Place the flour, yeast, salt and sugar in a mixing bowl and blend together until well amalgamated. Add the cubes of butter to the flour and rub in, but only very lightly as you still want fairly big chunks of butter – about 5mm in size.

3 Pour the cold water and milk mixture into the flour and gently bring together to a fairly scraggy ball. Tip this out on to the counter and clump together. Take care not to melt the chunks of butter as they need to stay firm.

4 Flour the worktop and a rolling pin. Roll the pastry out into a long thin rectangle – about 12cm wide, and as long as it becomes when about 1cm thick. Brush excess flour from the pastry with a pastry brush. Fold the two ends so they meet in the centre; brush excess flour off, then fold these doubled-up ends together like a book (this is called the 'book fold'.) Turn the dough a quarter turn and roll it away from you into a long rectangle again. Fold again as above, then wrap in baking paper and chill in the fridge for an hour.

5 Remove from the fridge and repeat the rolling and book fold again, wrap in cling film and chill in the fridge overnight, or preferably 24 hours.

6 In the morning, or after the chilling time, remove from the fridge and complete one final roll and fold. The pastry is now ready to be used as the recipe requires.

RICH SWEET SHORTCRUST PASTRY
MAKES ABOUT 500G

1 egg
125g golden caster sugar
1 tsp vanilla or almond extract
250g plain flour
125g salted butter, in 1cm cubes

Essential equipment
Butter knife or pastry cutter

I adore this pastry. It is sweet and crispy and so perfect for making tarts, be they delicate, French-inspired tarts or robust, pie-like ones. Due to the sugar in the pastry, it browns much quicker than an ordinary shortcrust, and so is best baked at a lower temperature.

1 Place the egg, sugar and vanilla or almond in a mixing bowl, and whisk – I use a balloon whisk – for a minute, or until the sugar is dissolved into the egg.

2 Sift the flour into the mixture and stir in using a wooden spoon, until the mixture has a sandy texture – be sure to scrape around the bottom of the bowl so there are no clumps of flour.

3 Add the cubed butter, and cut in using a butter knife or a pastry cutter until the butter is well incorporated and the dough comes together. (This pastry gets too sticky too quickly to do this by hand, which is why you use a knife or cutter.) Remove from the bowl and knead gently for a few seconds. Wrap in baking paper and chill for at least 30 minutes before using.

HOT WATER CRUST PASTRY
MAKES ABOUT 550G

250g plain flour
50g wholemeal flour
1 tsp salt
120ml water
100g lard
1 tbsp olive oil
A dash of Worcestershire sauce

This is a pastry that defies the usual 'light touch and cold hands' maxim (though, to be honest, I have very hot hands and make pastry just fine). This requires hot water and melted fats – the complete opposite to a delicate shortcrust. The result is a much bolder pastry, perfect for encasing meats.

1 Place the flours and salt in a heatproof bowl and stir together with a wooden spoon.

2 Put the water, lard, oil and Worcestershire sauce in a saucepan over a high heat and bring to the boil. When the liquid is boiling ferociously and the lard is melted, remove

from the heat and allow to cool for a minute, then pour it into the flour. Stir the contents of the bowl together with a wooden spoon until it all comes together in a thick, greasy pastry.

3 When the liquids have become absorbed into the flour, it should be just cool enough to use your hands, so do so. Knead the pastry together on the worktop for a minute or so until it is smooth and doughy. Use as described in the recipe.

PISTACHIO PASTE
MAKES 300G

250g best quality, unshelled pistachios
   (the greener the better)
50g golden caster sugar

This is a gorgeous green paste – quite a thick paste at that. Its flavour is purely pistachio, and it is marvellous in cake batters and mousseline. I've given you this recipe so you can have a bash at my Raspberry and Pistachio Genoise Slices on page 77. You will need a food processor for this – the small, 'baby-food' sized bowl. You can also make this with other nuts if you are creating your own recipes.

1 Put the pistachios and sugar into the food processor and blitz on full speed for about 5 minutes, then give the food processor a 5-minute break so it doesn't overheat. Scrape the pistachios down from the side of the bowl if necessary. Repeat this process of blitzing and pausing until the pistachios come together in a very thick paste. This could take between 15 and 40 minutes, so be patient and don't let your processor overheat.

2 When you have the paste, wrap it in cling film and form it into a sausage. Store in the fridge.

MIRROR GLAZE
FOR 1 CAKE

1 gelatine leaf
120g golden caster sugar
60ml water
1 tbsp golden syrup
75g cocoa powder
60ml single cream

I'm obsessed with this glaze. It has to be the most impressive thing you can put on top of a cake, especially a chocolate cake. Thanks to the gelatine and the golden syrup, the glaze sets shiny; it doesn't lose its shine as a ganache tends to. To use this, it needs to be melted so it can be poured in a steady stream on the bake. Scoop it out into a jug and microwave it on medium for 30-second bursts until it is liquid. This keeps perfectly well in the fridge for a week or two.

1 Soak the gelatine leaf in a bowl of cold water for 5 minutes.

2 Heat the sugar, water and golden syrup in a small saucepan. Allow to boil for a minute or two, then remove from the heat and whisk in the cocoa powder. Whisk in the cream, then return to a medium heat for a minute, stirring constantly. Remove from the heat.

3 Take the gelatine leaf from the bowl, squeeze to remove excess water, add to the chocolate glaze and stir until dissolved. Pass the glaze through a sieve into a bowl. Store in the fridge until needed.

EXPRESS LIME CURD
MAKES ABOUT 500G

250ml fresh lime juice, plus 1–2 tablespoons
125g unsalted butter, cut into cubes
Zest of 1 lime
3 egg yolks
175g golden caster sugar
25g cornflour

Making curd can be tedious: standing by the stove stirring a bowl for what feels like hours, especially when you're in a bit of a rush! Another option is the microwave, but that can be too powerful. It was only recently, when I was making a batch of crème pâtissière, that I thought of an easier way to do it. Now I make curd using the same method as crème pâtissière and it really does work a treat. This recipe is quite sharp, which I love, and it is perfect for my Mojito Cake (see page 146), but if you want it sweeter, just up the sugar to 225g. This method would also work using the same quantity of lemon, orange or even passion fruit pulp, blended and sieved.

1 Place the lime juice, butter and zest in a medium saucepan and heat over a medium-high heat.

2 Meanwhile, whisk together the yolks and caster sugar – adding a tablespoon of lime juice if it's a little thick – then whisk in the cornflour.

3 When the butter melts into the lime juice and it comes to the boil, pour half on to the eggs and sugar, whisking constantly to blend, then pour that into the remaining butter and lime juice in the pan and heat again, whisking constantly until the mixture thickens and coats the back of a spoon. Take the pan off the heat so that it doesn't thicken or split while you are testing.

4 Scoop it on to a plate, allow to cool, then cover with cling film to chill, or put into a sterilized jar with a lid.

VANILLA CREME PATISSIERE
MAKES ABOUT 800G

4 egg yolks
125g golden caster sugar
40g cornflour
500ml milk
1 vanilla pod, halved lengthways,
  or 1 tsp vanilla paste or extract
40g unsalted butter

The staple of French baking. Confectioner's custard with a French accent.

1 Place the egg yolks and caster sugar in a mixing bowl and whisk until the sugar is dissolved and the mixture is slightly paler in colour.

2 Add the cornflour and whisk well so there are no lumps of flour left. Place the bowl on a folded, dampened tea towel in readiness for the next stage.

3 Put the milk in a medium saucepan along with the vanilla and place over a medium-high heat until just before the milk boils. Pour half this milk into the bowl with the eggs, whisking continuously as you do so; the dampened tea towel helps stop the bowl sliding around.

4 When the milk is well incorporated into the eggs, pour it all back into the remaining milk in the saucepan and return to a medium-high heat, whisking constantly until the mixture is bubbling gently and is thick enough to coat the back of a spoon, barely dripping off. This will take 3–4 minutes.

5 Remove from the heat, continue to whisk for a minute more, then add the butter, stirring until it is melted into the crème pâtissière. Remove the vanilla pod, if you used one. Pour the crème pâtissière into a bowl, allow to cool briefly, then cover the surface with cling film (to prevent a skin forming) and refrigerate until needed. Use within a week.

CARDAMOM CREME PATISSIERE

Add 10 bruised cardamom pods to the milk, heat it slightly, then allow it to infuse for an hour. Continue as above, leaving the cardamom pods in the crème pâtissière, but make sure you remove them before using in a recipe.

MOUSSELINE CREME PATISSIERE

Above recipe completely made, plus 250g unsalted butter, softened. Take the cooled, set crème pâtissière and beat it in a freestanding electric mixer with whisk attachment, or in a mixing bowl with handheld electric whisk. Slowly add the softened butter a little at a time, and continue whisking until all the butter is incorporated and the mixture is smooth.

INDEX

ACKNOWLEDGEMENTS

A BOOK DOESN'T WRITE ITSELF, YOU KNOW. AND THE NAME ON THE SPINE IS MERELY ONE PERSON OUT OF A GREAT HANDFUL. FIRSTLY, THANK YOU TO MARI. YOUR FORENSIC APPROACH IS PERFECT, AND FOR IT I'M SO GRATEFUL. SARAH, VICKY AND ALL AT HEADLINE. THANK YOU AGAIN, SO VERY MUCH. STUART AND CLAIRE AT METROSTAR. THANKS EVER SO MUCH FOR SIMPLY EVERYTHING. JONNY AND ROX, I CAN'T TELL YOU HOW MUCH I APPRECIATE EVERYTHING. AND HOLLY ARNOLD, YOU'RE THE ICING ON THE CAKE. EMMA AND ALEX, ZOE AND LISA (AND, OF COURSE, PEPPER), THANK YOU FOR ALL THE FUN. OH, AND AN INCREDIBLE DESIGN. MANY THANKS TO TAMZIN FOR PICKING PERFECT PROPS. MATT RUSSELL, JUST, WOW. YOU AND YOUR PHOTOGRAPHS ARE LOVELY. SUSIE 'ET' BRADY, THANKS FOR KEEPING THE NORTHERN FUN GOING. RICHARD HARRIS. YOU'RE A FABULOUS FOODIE AND A FABULOUS FRIEND. THANKS ALSO TO KATY ROSS AND VIC GRIER FOR EXCELLENT WORK. ANNIE RIGG (AND MUNGO), I'M HONOURED YOU WORKED ON THE BOOK, THANKS.

THANKS TO NIKKI MORGAN, LEYNAH AND KATIE AT SILVER SPOON, ELISA AT LE CREUSET, SARAH ET AL AT WILD CARD, KATE, GEN AND SARAH AT NUDGE, MARCUS AT NORDICWARE, PERVEEN FROM INTEL. YOUR CONSTANT SUPPORT HAS BEEN OVERWHELMING. I'M SORRY IF I'VE MISSED ANYONE OUT. THANKS, HOLLY, ALEX, DAN, LYDIA AND BEN FOR TREKKING TO WEST LONDON TO CAMEO IN THIS BOOK. SUSAN RAE, YOU ARE A BEACON OF SANITY IN A VERY MAD CITY (OR IS THAT A BEACON OF MADNESS IN AN OVERLY SANE CITY?). I'M ENDLESSLY GRATEFUL TO ALL AT LOVE – STILL HASN'T SUNK IN. I'M IMMENSELY INDEBTED TO CHEFS JULIE, GRAHAM, NICHOLAS AND ALL AT LE CORDON BLEU FOR TEACHING ME TO BE A PROFESSIONAL AND FOR AMPLIFYING MY PASSION. AND, OF COURSE, TO LARRY, TO WHOM I AM ETERNALLY GRATEFUL. TO PAUL, YOU ROCK MY WORLD (AND YOU'RE FAB AT CLEANING THE KITCHEN). AND TO OUR FAMILY, WITHOUT WHICH WE'D BE LOST IN SPACE.